THE UNOFFICIAL COOKBOOK FOR
NINJA FOODI
BEGINNERS

THE UNOFFICIAL COOKBOOK FOR NINJA FOODI BEGINNERS

A Healthy Guide to Using the Pressure Cooker That Crisps

James O. Fraioli

Recipes by Tiffany Fraioli

Skyhorse Publishing

Skyhorse Publishing books may be purchased in bulk at special discounts for sales promotion, corporate gifts, fund-raising, or educational purposes. Special editions can also be created to specifications. For details, contact the Special Sales Department, Skyhorse Publishing, 307 West 36th Street, 11th Floor, New York, NY 10018 or info@skyhorsepublishing.com.

Skyhorse® and Skyhorse Publishing® are registered trademarks of Skyhorse Publishing, Inc.®, a Delaware corporation.

Visit our website at www.skyhorsepublishing.com.

10 9 8 7 6 5 4 3 2 1

Library of Congress Cataloging-in-Publication Data is available on file.

Cover design by Kai Texel
Cover photo credit: Tucker + Hossler

Print ISBN: 978-1-5107-5548-2
Ebook ISBN: 978-1-5107-5549-9

Printed in the United States of America

THANK-YOUS

The author would like to personally thank Nicole Frail and the wonderful team at Skyhorse Publishing; Hattie May Root, Taira Poletz, Jackson Poletz, Laura Scherer, Ed Geric, Carolyn Harries-Duncan, Gordon Duncan, Eric Rudd, William Rudd, Tucker + Hossler Photography, and Tiffany Fraioli for her incredible assistance and culinary expertise.

CONTENTS

INTRODUCTION

Welcome to the Ninja Foodi.

As you've probably heard, the Ninja Foodi is revolutionizing the home cooking and multi-cooker industry. This amazing and robust kitchen appliance with two unique lids and a straightforward control panel starts as a pressure cooker to lock in flavor and make your foods more tender while speeding up the cooking process by up to 70 percent compared to most traditional cooking methods. The Ninja then quickly converts over to a broiler using TenderCrisp cooking technology, the first of its kind, so you can finish your dishes with crisp and crunch using little to no oil. Some call the Ninja Foodi pressure cooking and air-crisping in one pot. Others call it a culinary miracle.

Whether you choose the 6.5-quart model or larger 8-quart, the Ninja Foodi easily allows you to air-fry, dehydrate, steam, slow cook, sear, sauté, bake, roast, and broil, using fresh and/or frozen ingredients. These options are ideal for home cooks with busy schedules and hungry mouths to feed. In addition, Ninja Foodi's versatility means it's welcome in many small kitchens struggling for space or appliance overload. And when it comes to cleaning, the Ninja Foodi is just as convenient. Nonstick cooking surfaces and dishwasher-safe parts and accessories make cleanup a breeze.

In the pages ahead, you will quickly become familiar with the Ninja Foodi. You'll be introduced to the two types of cooking lids along with the various control and function buttons on the easy-to-use panel. You'll discover the many accessories you can add to the Ninja Foodi while instructions on proper care, cleaning, and safety precautions when using the appliance will guide you along the way. Then there are the recipes. More than 75 of them.

The recipes are straightforward and, with a few exceptions, focus on the healthy side of eating. These wholesome dishes include relatively easy-to-find ingredients with minimal cooking steps. Whether you're assembling a Denver omelet and blistering Brussels sprouts, or roasting chicken and baking zucchini bread, the Ninja Foodi's quick and easy methods will have you serving up delicious meals for your friends and family in no time. So, what are you waiting for? Turn the pages ahead and begin your gastronomic journey into the magical world of the Ninja Foodi.

THE NINJA FOODI

GETTING FAMILIAR WITH THE NINJA FOODI

When you first unpack your Ninja Foodi box, you will discover the exciting Ninja Foodi appliance along with an assortment of cooking accessories.

- **Ninja Foodi with attached Crisping Lid**
- **Pressure Lid**
- **Removable Cooking Pot** (must always be inserted when the Ninja Foodi is in use)
- **Cook and Crisp Basket** (with detachable diffuser)
- **Reversible Rack** (with Lower position for steaming and Higher position for broil)
- **Cook and Crisping Layered Insert**

Many of the wonderful recipes that follow in the pages ahead will refer to the Ninja Foodi and the accessories above. Please familiarize yourself with each component before attempting the recipes.

LIDS

Why Two Ninja Foodi Cooking Lids?

There are two lids that come with the Ninja Foodi. They are the pressure lid and the crisping lid. The two-lid design allows you to pressure-cook and crisp in the same pot, which is what makes the Ninja Foodi so revolutionary.

Lid

Pressure Lid

The pressure lid is used to tenderize the food when pressure-cooking, steaming, slow cooking, and searing/sautéing. The recipes will indicate when to use this lid.

Note: When removing the pressure lid, always lift and tilt away from you while making sure no condensation drips into the cooker base.

There are also two types of pressure releases the recipes will refer to when using the pressure lid. They are natural pressure release and quick pressure release. The recipes will indicate what pressure release to use.

Natural Pressure Release

After pressure-cooking is complete, the steam inside the Ninja Foodi will naturally release from the appliance as it cools down. This can take up to twenty minutes. During this time, the appliance will automatically switch to KEEP WARM mode. When the natural pressure release is finished, the red float valve on the appliance will drop down.

Quick Pressure Release

Some recipes call for the quick pressure release. To release quickly, turn the pressure-release valve from the SEAL position to the VENT position, and the pressure inside the Ninja Foodi will be released immediately.

At any time during natural pressure release, you can switch to quick pressure release by simply turning the pressure-release valve to VENT.

Crisping Lid

The crisping lid is used to crisp the food when air-crisping, baking, roasting, broiling, and dehydrating. Unlike the pressure lid, the crisping lid is attached to the Ninja Foodi by a hinge and features an easy-open design. The lid can be open during any cooking method that calls for the crisping lid. This is an excellent feature when needing to check on the food during the cooking process. The recipes will indicate when to use this lid.

Pressure-release valve

Crisping lid

Control panel

Function Buttons

There are eight basic functions of the Ninja Foodi. They are:

- **Pressure**: Quickly cooks food.
- **Steam**: Gently cooks food at high temperature.
- **Slow Cook**: Cooks food at low temperature for longer period of time.
- **Sear/Sauté**: Acts as a stovetop to brown meats, sauté vegetables, etc.
- **Air Crisp**: Gives food crispiness and crunch without the use of little or no oil.
- **Bake/Roast**: Acts as an oven to cook meat, bake desserts, etc.
- **Broil**: To caramelize and brown food under the burner.
- **Dehydrate**: Dehydrating meats, fruits and vegetables for healthy treats.

Let's quickly look at each function so you are familiar with them before attempting the recipes.

Pressure

This requires the pressure lid and turning the pressure-release valve to SEAL.

As pressure builds inside the Ninja Foodi, the control panel will display rotating lights. As the appliance pressurizes, the lid will safely lock and will not unlock until the pressure is released. Once the appliance has reached full pressure, the lid icon light will illuminate. The pressure-cooking cycle will then begin, and the timer will start counting down, based on the amount of cooking time you entered.

Pressure can be adjusted from low to high, depending on the particular recipe.

Steam

Sear/sauté

Steam

When steaming, you will use the reversible rack in the lower position while following the same instructions as above. However, pressure cannot be adjusted from low to high during steaming.

Slow Cook

To slow cook, follow the same instruction as given for the pressure function above.

Air Crisp

When air-crisping, you will be using the cook and crisp basket. The crisping lid will always be in the closed position, and the temperature and minute buttons should be set according to the temperature and amount of time the particular recipe calls for. You will be able to safely lift the crisping lid while cooking to check on your food.

Sear/Sauté

With the SEAR/SAUTÉ function, no lid is necessary, and the recipes will remind you of this. There is also no time adjustment with this function. You simply press START/STOP to begin.

Broil

When broiling, you will use the reversible rack in the higher position while following the same instructions above. However, temperature cannot be adjusted during broiling.

Bake/roast

Bake/Roast

Similar to air-crisping, when baking and roasting, the crisping lid will always be in the closed position, and the temperature and minute buttons should be set according to the temperature and amount of time the particular recipe calls for. You will be able to safely lift the crisping lid while cooking to check on your food.

Dehydrate

Similar to air-crisping, you will be using the cook and crisp basket or dehydrating rack (see Accessories, page 7) when dehydrating. The crisping lid will always be in the closed position, and the temperature and minute buttons should be set according to the temperature and amount of time the dehydrating recipe calls for.

NOTES

_____

_____

_____

_____

_____

_____

_____

Operating Buttons

TEMP Arrows

Use the up and down TEMP arrows to raise and lower temperature levels and/or pressure level (low and high).

TIME Arrows

Use the up and down TIME arrows to increase or decrease the cooking time.

START/STOP

Press the START/STOP button after selecting the temperature (or pressure) and cooking time. Press to start cooking. Press again and the appliance will stop.

KEEP WARM

After cooking, the appliance will automatically switch to KEEP WARM, and the built-in time will begin counting up. The KEEP WARM function will stay on for twelve hours, or until you press KEEP WARM to turn it off.

Power and Standby

The power button turns the appliance off when pressed and stops all cooking.

If the control panel is not used after the appliance has been turned on for 10 minutes, the appliance will automatically switch to STANDBY.

For additional operation instructions and to learn more about the Ninja Foodi functions, please consult your Ninja Foodi Owner's Guide, or go online at: ninjakitchen.com.

NINJA FOODI ACCESSORIES

There are a variety of fun accessories on the market, which are cleverly designed to help make your Ninja Foodi experience more efficient and rewarding.

Here's a list of some of those popular customized accessories, which are sold separately and which you should consider purchasing if you find yourself cooking regularly with the Ninja Foodi:

Crisper Pan

Need to reheat the dishes you made from the Ninja Foodi? Forget the microwave and instead use this pan, which will heat your food and keep it crispy thanks to the increased airflow from the pan's perforated holes.

Dehydrating Rack

Ready to start making your own beef or salmon jerky? What about drying that extra fruit from your backyard orchard or transforming leftover vegetables from your garden into crispy chips? With this clever device, including its five stackable layers, you'll be able to dehydrate at home in no time.

Egg Bite Mold

The seven-mold design allows you to bake items in an individual manner such as mini-muffins, egg bites, personal cakes, pudding, and more. Because it's made from silicone, make sure never to use the mold above 450°F.

Kitchen Tongs

One of the most popular kitchen tools on the market. Great for all types of cooking with the Ninja Foodi. Invest in both a short and long pair, and make sure the tongs are high-heat resistant.

Loaf Pan

This 8-inch pan is designed specifically for baking breads or cooking meatloaf in the Ninja Foodi.

Multipurpose Pan

Similar to the loaf pan, this round 8-inch pan is the perfect pan when baking cakes and desserts.

Nonstick Springform Pan

This 7-inch pan is what you need if you're baking cakes that cannot withstand being flipped upside down for pan removal. With a lateral latch, you'll be able to release your most delicate dessert creations.

Oven Mitts

A must when lifting scalding hot pots, racks, and pans out of the Ninja Foodi. Save yourself the burns by investing in a pair of these small silicone mitts.

Plate Gripper

As an alternative to the oven mitts, this tool allows you to lift hot dishes safely without burning yourself.

Roasting Rack Insert

With its perfect upright design, this insert, which gets placed inside the cook and crisp basket, is ideal when heating taco shells, cooking ribs, or crisping bread.

Silicone Pad

These heat insulation pads come in handy when needing to set down hot dishes on the counter or dinner table.

Silicone pads

Silicone Rings

These rings are the rubber seals that fit inside the cooking lids. Purchase an extra two-pack of silicone rings if you would like to keep your flavors separate. For example, use one ring when cooking savory and spicy foods, then replace with a separate ring when cooking sweets and desserts. See page 10 for how to remove and reinstall the silicone rings.

Silicone Scrubber

Smaller in shape than the silicone pad, these little guys are ideal for scrubbing fruits and vegetables as well as cleaning the Ninja Foodi accessories.

Skewer Stand

A rack that holds fifteen skewers (included); enough to make a wide assortment of kebabs for your next dinner party. Please know this stand only works with the larger, 8-quart Ninja Foodi removable cooking pot.

Stackable Egg Rack

This multifunction rack serves as an egg rack and steamer rack and is great for lifting plates and bowls off the surface.

Steamer Basket

This versatile basket is both a colander and a steamer. It's great for straining, too. Need to boil a dozen eggs or steam a platter of asparagus, broccoli, or seafood for your next gathering? This large basket is a must.

Steamer Rack

With tall handles on each side, this ingenious rack design allows you to lift pans, molds, and containers out of the Ninja Foodi with ease.

CARE AND CLEANING

As with any kitchen appliance, proper care, maintenance, and cleaning will lead to many enjoyable years of cooking with the Ninja Foodi.

After each use, the appliance should be thoroughly cleaned. To properly do so, always unplug the appliance before cleaning. NEVER place the Ninja Foodi, lids, or base into the dishwasher or immerse them in water or dishwashing liquid.

To clean the Ninja Foodi, including the crisping lid, pressure lid with pressure-release valve, and the base, simply wipe down with a soft, nonabrasive damp kitchen cloth or towel. If food residue is stuck on particular areas, you can use a little nonabrasive liquid dish soap.

Parts such as the cooking pot, silicone ring, reversible rack, cook and crisp basket, the detachable diffuser, and most Ninja Foodi accessories can be gently washed in dishwater. When in doubt, wash by hand, and never use harsh scouring pads, as they will scratch the Ninja Foodi and its various components and parts.

When finished cleaning, air-dry all the parts before reusing the appliance.

CLEANING THE ANTI-CLOG CAP

The anti-clog cap is located on the underside of the pressure lid. This cap protects the inner valve of the pressure-release valve from clogging and potential food splatters when the lid is removed. This cap should be cleaned with a small cleaning brush after every use. To remove the cap, simply squeeze and pull upward. To reinstall, place the cap back in its original position and press down.

REMOVING AND REINSTALLING THE SILICONE RINGS

To remove, exchange, or replace the silicone rings, simply pull the ring outward, section by section, from the ring rack. To reinstall, press the ring into the rack, section by section, just like when you removed the ring.

It is important to always keep the silicone ring clean to avoid odor from cooking various foods. It's best to order extra silicone rings so you can change them depending on what you're cooking, thereby keeping the flavors separate.

To clean the silicone ring, wash by hand or in the dishwasher.

Replace the silicone ring if it begins to crack or have any cuts or nicks. Always replace a damaged ring immediately.

SAFETY FIRST

Always read the Ninja Foodi's Owner's Manual before using the appliance. When cooking with the Ninja Foodi, basic safety precautions should also be used, including:

DO NOT use an extension cord or automatic timer with the Ninja Foodi.

DO NOT use the Ninja Foodi outdoors, or in moving vehicles or boats.

DO NOT use the Ninja Foodi without the provided removable cooking pot in place.

DO NOT use the Ninja Foodi to cook instant rice.

DO NOT touch hot surfaces of the Ninja Foodi; always use protective pads and/or oven mitts, and always use the handles and knobs on the appliance.

DO NOT use the Ninja Foodi on uneven surfaces; the surface should always be clean, dry, and level.

DO NOT use the Ninja Foodi near hot gas, hot surfaces, or electric burner's or in a heated oven.

DO NOT use the Ninja Foodi cooking pot, racks, or any Ninja Foodi parts in the microwave, gas range, oven, or outdoor grill.

DO NOT use the Ninja Foodi pressure-cooking function with a loose-fitting or unlocked pressure lid. Always make sure the pressure lid is properly assembled and locked into position before use.

DO NOT immerse the Ninja Foodi cord, base, or crisping lid in water or other liquid.

DO NOT rinse the Ninja Foodi under running water.

DO NOT cover the Ninja Foodi pressure valves located on the pressure lid.

DO NOT move the Ninja Foodi when in use.

DO NOT use the Ninja Foodi if the silicone rings are cut, torn, or damaged.

DO NOT use the Ninja Foodi to sauté or fry with oil while pressure-cooking.

DO NOT use the slow cook function on the Ninja Foodi without food or liquid in the cooking pot.

DO NOT use the Ninja Foodi for deep-frying.

DO NOT overfill the Ninja Foodi when cooking.

DO NOT use the Ninja Foodi to pressure-cook if the red float valve is clogged or obstructed. Always make sure the valve is clean and moves freely.

DO NOT attempt to open the pressure lid during or after pressure-cooking until all internal pressure has been released through the pressure-release valve and the unit has cooled slightly.

DO NOT ever force the cooking lids to open or close.

DO NOT use a damaged removable cooking pot or lid.

DO NOT stand over the pressure-release valve prior to or during the pressure release.

FEEDING YOUR *FOODI* FRIENDS AND FAMILY: RECIPES

Fresh Starts

AVOCADO AND EGGS WITH GRAPE TOMATOES

SERVES 2

3 EGG WHITES

2 RIPE AVOCADOS, CUT IN HALF
AND PITS REMOVED

2 GRAPE TOMATOES, HALVED

SALT, TO TASTE

FRESH CRACKED BLACK PEPPER,
TO TASTE

Close the crisping lid. Allow the appliance to preheat by selecting BAKE/ROAST, and set the temperature to 350°F and the time to 5 minutes. Select START/STOP to begin.

In a bowl, whisk the egg whites, then pour equal amounts into each avocado depression where the pit was removed. Do not overflow. Top each depression with a grape tomato half and season with salt and pepper.

Open the crisping lid and place the reversible rack into the cooking pot, making certain the rack is at the lower position. Carefully place the egg-filled avocados on top of the rack.

Close the crisping lid. Select BAKE/ROAST and set the temperature to 350°F and the time to 30 minutes, or until desired doneness. Select START/STOP to begin.

When cooking is finished, open the crisping lid and remove the avocados. Serve warm.

BAKED DENVER OMELET

SERVES 6 TO 8

8 EGGS

½ CUP LOW-FAT MILK

SALT, TO TASTE

FRESH CRACKED BLACK PEPPER,
   TO TASTE

1 CUP LOW-FAT SHREDDED
   CHEDDAR CHEESE

1 CUP LOW-SODIUM COOKED
   SMOKED HAM, DICED

⅓ CUP RED BELL PEPPER,
   SEEDED AND DICED

⅓ CUP GREEN BELL PEPPER,
   SEEDED AND DICED

2 TABLESPOONS ONION, PEELED
   AND CHOPPED

Close the crisping lid. Allow the appliance to preheat by selecting BAKE/ROAST, and set the temperature to 350°F and the time to 5 minutes. Select START/STOP to begin.

In a large bowl, add the eggs, milk, salt, and pepper. Whisk until eggs are liquified, then add the cheese, ham, bell peppers, and onion. Grease an 8-inch baking pan and pour the egg mixture into the pan. Next, place the pan on top of the reversible rack.

After 5 minutes, open the crisping lid and place the pan and reversible rack into the cooking pot, making certain the rack is at the lower position. Close the lid. Select BAKE/ROAST and set the temperature to 315°F and the time to 35 minutes. Select START/STOP to begin.

After 35 minutes, remove the pan and serve the omelet immediately.

BAKED HAM, CHILE, AND CHEESE OMELET

SERVES 6 TO 8

8 EGGS

½ CUP LOW-FAT MILK

SALT, TO TASTE

FRESH CRACKED BLACK PEPPER,
   TO TASTE

1 CUP LOW-FAT SHREDDED
   CHEDDAR CHEESE

1 CUP LOW-SODIUM COOKED
   SMOKED HAM, DICED

4 OUNCES CANNED DICED GREEN
   CHILES

Close the crisping lid. Allow the appliance to preheat by selecting BAKE/ROAST, and setting the temperature to 350°F and the time to 5 minutes. Select START/STOP to begin.

In a large bowl, add the eggs, milk, salt, and pepper. Whisk until eggs are liquified, then add the cheese, ham, and chiles. Grease an 8-inch baking pan and pour the egg mixture into the pan. Next, place the pan on top of the reversible rack.

After 5 minutes, open the crisping lid and place the pan and reversible rack into the cooking pot, making certain the rack is at the lower position. Close the lid. Select BAKE/ROAST and set the temperature to 315°F and the time to 35 minutes. Select START/STOP to begin.

After 35 minutes, remove the pan and serve the omelet immediately.

BAKED MUSHROOM AND GOAT CHEESE OMELET WITH SPINACH AND AVOCADO

SERVES 6 TO 8

3–4 TABLESPOONS GRAPESEED OIL

8–9 OUNCES MUSHROOMS OF CHOICE, SLICED

8 EGGS

½ CUP LOW-FAT MILK

SALT, TO TASTE

FRESH CRACKED BLACK PEPPER, TO TASTE

3 CUPS BABY SPINACH

6 TABLESPOONS CRUMBLED GOAT CHEESE

2 RIPE AVOCADOS, PITTED, PEELED, AND DICED

FRESH ITALIAN FLAT-LEAF PARSLEY, FOR GARNISH

Preheat the appliance for 5 minutes by selecting SEAR/SAUTÉ and setting to HIGH. Press START/STOP to begin. Note: You will not be using a lid until instructed.

Add the oil to the cooking pot and heat. Add the mushrooms and sauté for 5 minutes, or until mushrooms are brown and tender. Remove from pot and set aside.

In a large bowl, add the eggs, milk, salt, and pepper. Whisk until the eggs are liquified, then add the sautéed mushrooms, spinach, goat cheese, and diced avocado. Grease an 8-inch baking pan and pour the egg mixture into the pan. Next, place the pan on top of the reversible rack.

Place the pan and reversible rack into the cooking pot, making certain the rack is at the lower position. Close the crisping lid. Select BAKE/ROAST and set the temperature to 315°F and the time to 35 minutes. Select START/STOP to begin.

After 35 minutes, remove the pan and serve the omelet immediately with a sprinkling of fresh parsley.

CINNAMON FRENCH TOAST

SERVES 2

4 EGGS

2 TEASPOONS CINNAMON

2 TEASPOONS VANILLA EXTRACT

½ CUP LOW-FAT MILK

6 SLICES PEPPERIDGE FARM
   BROWN SUGAR–CINNAMON
   SWIRL BREAD

PURE MAPLE SYRUP, AS NEEDED

TURKEY BACON, (OPTIONAL;
   PAGE 29)

In a large mixing bowl, add the eggs, cinnamon, vanilla, and milk. Whisk together well until the eggs are liquified.

Soak each piece of bread in the egg mixture, until both sides are well coated.

Transfer the bread slices to an 8-inch greased baking pan. Note: If bread slices are too large, cut or cube the bread to fit. Place the pan on the reversible rack and set into the cooking pot, in the higher position.

Close the crisping lid. Select BAKE/ROAST and set the temperature to 325°F and the time to 8 minutes. Select START/STOP to begin.

Remove the pan and serve the cinnamon french toast with warm maple syrup and crisp turkey bacon, if desired.

COUNTRY HASH WITH EGGS

SERVES 4 TO 6

½ POUND LOW-SODIUM SMOKED
   HAM, DICED

2 TABLESPOONS VEGETABLE OIL

1 WHITE ONION, PEELED AND
   DICED

1 GREEN BELL PEPPER, SEEDED
   AND DICED

2 RUSSET POTATOES, PEELED
   (OPTIONAL), AND DICED

SALT, TO TASTE

FRESH CRACKED BLACK PEPPER,
   TO TASTE

4–6 EGGS

Preheat the appliance for 5 minutes by selecting SEAR/SAUTÉ and setting to HIGH. Press START/STOP to begin. Note: You will not be using a lid until instructed.

Add the ham to the cooking pot and sauté for 5 minutes, or until the ham is browned. Add the oil, onion, pepper, and potatoes. Season with salt and pepper. Sauté for 5 to 10 minutes, or until the onions are translucent and peppers are tender. Cook for 5 additional minutes, and do not stir to brown the vegetables. Then, stir the mixture and cook for another 5 minutes, this time without stirring. Crack the eggs onto the top of the hash, and season the eggs with salt and pepper.

Close the crisping lid. Select BROIL and set the time to 10 minutes. Select START/STOP to begin. Cook the eggs until desired doneness, checking often.

Remove the eggs and hash and serve immediately.

HUEVOS RANCHEROS

SERVES 4

1 TABLESPOON + 2 TEASPOONS
VEGETABLE OIL, DIVIDED

1 WHITE ONION, PEELED AND
DICED

3 CLOVES GARLIC, PEELED AND
CHOPPED

16 OUNCES BLACK BEANS,
RINSED

3 TEASPOONS SALT, DIVIDED

½ TEASPOON CUMIN

¼ CUP WATER

6 EGGS

½ CUP CRUMBLED QUESO
FRESCO, DIVIDED

4 CORN TOSTADAS, WARMED

1 CUP PICO DE GALLO

1 RIPE AVOCADO, PITTED,
PEELED, AND SLICED

¼ CUP FRESH CILANTRO,
CHOPPED

Preheat the appliance for 5 minutes by selecting SEAR/SAUTÉ and setting to HIGH. Press START/STOP to begin. Note: You will not be using a lid until instructed.

Add 1 tablespoon oil to the cooking pot and heat. Add the onion and sauté for 3 minutes. Add the garlic and sauté for 1 minute. Next, add the beans, 1 teaspoon salt, cumin, and water. Stir well.

Secure the pressure lid and turn the pressure-release valve to the SEAL position. Select PRESSURE and set to HIGH. Set time to 3 minutes. Press START/STOP to begin.

In a small bowl, add the eggs, ¼ cup cheese, and the remaining salt. Mix well to combine.

After 3 minutes, turn the pressure-release valve to the VENT position. Wait until the pressure has been released, then remove the pressure lid.

Remove the beans from the pot, and lightly mash with a fork.

Select SEAR/SAUTÉ and set to MEDIUM-HIGH. Press START/STOP to begin. Add the remaining oil and the egg mixture. Note: You will not be using a lid during this step.

Stir the eggs until scrambled, about 3 minutes. Remove the eggs.

To plate, spread the beans on the tostada, then arrange the eggs, salsa, and avocado on top. Garnish with the salsa, remaining cheese, and cilantro.

LEEK AND MUSHROOM FRITTATA

SERVES 6 TO 8

3 TABLESPOONS GRAPESEED OIL

2 LEEKS, WHITE AND LIGHT-
GREEN PARTS, THINLY SLICED

8 OUNCES WILD MUSHROOMS
SLICED

12 EGGS

½ CUP CRÈME FRAÎCHE

2 TABLESPOONS FRESH ITALIAN
FLAT-LEAF PARSLEY, MINCED

1 CUP LOW-FAT SHREDDED
CHEDDAR OR SWISS CHEESE,
DIVIDED

¼ TEASPOON SALT

¼ TEASPOON FRESH CRACKED
BLACK PEPPER

1 CUP WATER

Preheat the appliance by selecting SEAR/SAUTÉ and setting to
MEDIUM-HIGH. Press START/STOP to begin and add the oil. Note:
You will not be using a lid until instructed.

After 5 minutes, the appliance should be preheated and the oil should
be hot, so add the leeks and cook for 5 minutes, or until soft. Add the
mushrooms, stirring often, until the liquid has evaporated. Remove
the leeks and mushrooms.

In a large bowl, add the eggs, crème fraîche, parsley, ¾ cup cheese,
salt, and pepper. Mix well until the eggs are liquified. Fold in the
sautéed leeks and mushrooms and add the water.

Grease an 8-inch baking pan and pour the egg mixture into the pan.
Next, place the pan on top of the reversible rack.

Place the pan and reversible rack into the cooking pot, making
certain the rack is at the lower position.

Secure the pressure lid and turn the pressure-release valve to the
SEAL position. Select PRESSURE and set to HIGH. Set the time to
10 minutes. Press START/STOP to begin.

After 10 minutes, allow the pressure to naturally release for another
10 minutes. Then, switch the valve to the VENT position. Wait until
the pressure has been released, then remove the pressure lid.

Add the remaining cheese to the top of the frittata.

Close the crisping lid and press BROIL to preheat. Set the time to
7 minutes. Press START/STOP to begin.

Remove the frittata from the pan and serve immediately.

RASPBERRY BREAKFAST BARS

SERVES 8

1 CUP ALL-PURPOSE FLOUR

1 CUP QUICK-COOKING ROLLED
  OATS

⅓ CUP BROWN SUGAR

¼ TEASPOON BAKING SODA

½ CUP UNSALTED BUTTER,
  SOFTENED

1 CUP RASPBERRY JAM

Close the crisping lid. Allow the appliance to preheat by selecting
BAKE/ROAST, and set the temperature to 325°F and the time to
5 minutes. Select START/STOP to begin.

In a mixing bowl, add the flour, oats, brown sugar, and baking soda.
Mix well until combined. Add the softened butter, a little at a time,
and continue to mix until the mixture resembles coarse crumbs.
Reserve 1 cup of the mixture and set aside.

Grease an 8-inch baking pan. Press the oat mixture into the pan.
Next, spread the raspberry jam evenly over the oat mixture. Add the
remaining 1 cup of the mixture evenly over the top.

Next, place the pan on top of the reversible rack. Open the crisping
lid and place the pan and reversible rack into the cooking pot, making
certain the rack is at the lower position.

Close the crisping lid. Select BAKE/ROAST and set the temperature
to 325°F and the time to 30 minutes. Select START/STOP to begin.

After 30 minutes, remove the pan and rack from the pot. Allow to
cool completely before removing and cutting the oats into breakfast
bars.

ROASTED ORANGES

SERVES 2

2 TABLESPOONS BROWN SUGAR

2 TEASPOONS AGAVE SYRUP

¼ TEASPOON GROUND
    CARDAMOM

¼ TEASPOON GROUND GINGER

4 LARGE NAVEL ORANGES,
    CHILLED

Close the crisping lid. Allow the appliance to preheat by selecting BROIL for 5 minutes. Select START/STOP to begin.

In a small bowl, add the brown sugar, agave syrup, cardamom, and ginger. Mix until well combined.

Cut the oranges in half. Using a sharp paring knife, loosen the edges of the orange flesh from the white pith. Then spread the brown sugar–agave mixture evenly over the orange halves.

Line the reversible rack with foil. Open the crisping lid and place the rack in the higher position inside the cooking pot. Place the orange halves on the foil-lined rack.

Close the crisping lid. Select BROIL and set the time to 7 minutes. Select START/STOP to begin. Check for doneness after 5 minutes.

When cooking is complete, let the oranges cool for 1 to 2 minutes to allow the caramelized sugar to set. Serve warm.

STEEL-CUT OATMEAL

SERVES 4

1 CUP STEEL-CUT OATS

1½ CUPS WATER

½ TEASPOON SALT

¼ CUP UNSALTED BUTTER

½ CUP BROWN SUGAR

Add the oats, water, and salt to the cooking pot. Stir well to combine.

In an 8-inch baking pan, mix together the butter and brown sugar. Cover with aluminum foil. Add the reversible rack to the pot in the higher position. Place the baking pan on top of the rack.

Secure the pressure lid and turn the pressure-release valve to the SEAL position. Select PRESSURE and set to LOW. Set the time to 10 minutes. Press START/STOP to begin.

After 10 minutes, allow the pressure to naturally release for 7 minutes. Then, switch the valve to the VENT position. Wait until the pressure has been released, then remove the pressure lid.

Remove the baking pan and stir the melted butter and brown sugar. Pour over the oats and stir well to combine.

Remove the oats and serve immediately.

TATER TOT BREAKFAST HASH

SERVES 4 TO 6

32 OUNCES FROZEN TATER TOTS

1 POUND COOKED TURKEY
   BACON (PAGE 29)

1 CUP LOW-FAT SHREDDED
   CHEDDAR CHEESE

4 EGGS

1 CUP LOW-FAT MILK

½ PACKET HIDDEN VALLEY®
   RANCH DRESSING MIX

Add the tater tots, bacon, and cheddar cheese to the cooking pot.

In a large mixing bowl, whisk the eggs, milk, and ranch dressing mix until eggs are liquified. Pour the egg mixture over the tater tots, bacon, and cheese. Stir to incorporate.

Close the crisping lid. Select AIR CRISP and set the temperature to 350°F and the time to 25 minutes. Select START/STOP to begin.

After 15 minutes, check for desired doneness. Cook for an additional 5 to 10 minutes, if necessary.

Remove the hash and serve immediately.

TURKEY BACON

SERVES 2 TO 4

5 TO 6 SLICES TURKEY BACON

Place the bacon slices in the cook and crisp basket, being careful not to overlap the slices.

Close the crisping lid. Select AIR CRISP and set the temperature to 360°F and the time to 12 minutes. Select START/STOP to begin.

After 12 minutes, check the bacon for desired crispness. Cook for an additional 1 to 3 minutes, if necessary.

Remove the bacon and serve.

YOGURT WITH VANILLA, HONEY, AND BLUEBERRIES

SERVES 8

1 GALLON LOW-FAT MILK

2 TABLESPOONS PLAIN YOGURT
WITH ACTIVE LIVE CULTURES

1 TABLESPOON VANILLA
EXTRACT

½ CUP HONEY

1 PINT FRESH OR FROZEN
BLUEBERRIES

Add the milk to the cooking pot.

Select SEAR/SAUTÉ and set to MEDIUM. Press START/STOP to begin. Heat the milk, stirring frequently so it doesn't burn. Note: You will not be using a lid until instructed. Press START/STOP to turn off the appliance.

Let the milk cool slightly, while still stirring frequently. Remove any film on the surface.

Add the yogurt to the pot and whisk until well incorporated with the milk.

Secure the pressure lid and turn the pressure-release valve to the VENT position. Let sit for 8 hours.

Remove the yogurt from the pot and transfer to a suitable container. Chill in refrigerator until cool, about 3 or 4 hours.

Add the vanilla, honey, and blueberries to the yogurt. Stir well to incorporate. Cover and place in the refrigerator until ready to serve. Will keep for about 10 days.

Quick Six Ingredients or Fewer

AIR-FRIED SHRIMP WONTONS

SERVES 6

12 OUNCES COLD-WATER
    SHRIMP, SHELLED AND
    FINELY CHOPPED
¼ CUP LOW-FAT MAYONNAISE
16 OUNCES LOW-FAT CREAM,
    SOFTENED
½ LEMON, ZESTED
½ TEASPOON OLD BAY®
    SEASONING
12 OUNCES WONTON WRAPPERS

In a mixing bowl, add the shrimp, mayonnaise, cream cheese, lemon zest, and Old Bay Seasoning. Mix well until combined.

Fill a small bowl with water. Place 1 heaping teaspoon of the shrimp mixture in the middle of each wonton wrapper. Dab your finger with water and moisten the edge of the wrapper. Fold one end of the wrapper over to the other side, pressing to seal the edge. The wonton should resemble a triangle. Next, fold the corners of the triangle together and seal, creating a crown shape. Repeat the process with the remaining wontons.

Transfer the shrimp wontons to the freezer for about 2 hours to set.

When ready to cook, remove the wontons, arrange half of them in the cook and crisp basket, and place basket in the cooking pot. Note: You will be cooking the wontons in batches.

Close the crisping lid and press AIR CRISP. Set the temperature to 390°F and the time to 15 minutes. Press START/STOP to begin.

After 10 minutes, open the lid and check the wontons. Remove if they are golden brown. Otherwise, continue to cook.

When cooking is complete, remove the wontons and repeat with the remaining wontons. Serve warm.

BLOOMING ONION

SERVES 2

1 LARGE SWEET ONION, PEELED

2 EGGS

2 TABLESPOONS LOW-FAT MILK

1 CUP ITALIAN BREAD CRUMBS

1 TEASPOON SMOKED PAPRIKA

1 TEASPOON GARLIC SALT

GRAPESEED OIL, AS NEEDED

Using a sharp knife, remove the top of the onion and place the cut side down. Starting from the base, cut downward in eight even slices all the way around, but do not cut all the way through. Place the onion in cold ice water for about two hours.

Next, in a small mixing bowl, whisk together the eggs and milk.

In separate bowl, combine the bread crumbs with the smoked paprika and garlic salt.

Carefully dry the onion with paper towels and coat the onion and petals with the egg wash. Then coat liberally in the seasoned bread crumbs, shaking off any excess.

Brush the cook and crisp basket with a little grapeseed oil and place the seasoned onion in the basket.

Close the crisping lid and press AIR CRISP. Set the temperature to 390°F and the time to 10 minutes. Press START/STOP to begin.

After 10 minutes, check the onion for doneness. If it's not crispy enough, cook for another 5 minutes.

Serve immediately with your desired dipping sauce.

BRUSSELS SPROUTS

SERVES 4

2 POUNDS BRUSSELS SPROUTS, CUT IN HALF

2 TABLESPOONS GRAPESEED OIL

2 TEASPOONS SALT

1 TEASPOON FRESH CRACKED BLACK PEPPER

1 PINCH RED PEPPER FLAKES

Place the cook and crisp basket into the cooking pot. Close the crisping lid and preheat the appliance by pressing AIR CRISP. Set the temperature to 390°F and the time to 5 minutes. Press START/STOP to begin.

In a large bowl, add the Brussels sprouts, and toss with the oil, salt, pepper, and red pepper flakes.

After 5 minutes, open the lid and add the seasoned Brussels sprouts to the basket. Close the crisping lid and press AIR CRISP. Set the temperature to 390°F and the time to 20 minutes. Press START/STOP to begin.

After 10 minutes, open the lid, and lift the basket. Shake or toss the Brussels sprouts to move them around. Lower the basket back into the pot and close the lid to resume cooking. For crispy Brussels sprouts, continue to cook for another 3 minutes after the allotted 20 minutes.

When cooking is finished, remove the Brussels sprouts, and serve immediately.

CAULIFLOWER STEAKS

SERVES 4

½ CUP WATER

1 HEAD CAULIFLOWER, LEAVES
REMOVED, CUT INTO FOUR
1-INCH STEAKS

¼ CUP GRAPESEED OIL

4 CLOVES GARLIC, PEELED AND
MINCED

½ CUP GRATED PARMESAN
CHEESE

SALT, TO TASTE

1 TABLESPOON FRESH ITALIAN
FLAT-LEAF PARSLEY,
CHOPPED

Pour the water into the cooking pot.

Carefully place the cauliflower steaks into the cook and crisp basket and place the basket in the pot.

Secure the pressure lid and turn the pressure-release valve to the SEAL position.

Select PRESSURE and set to LOW. Set the time to 3 minutes. Press START/STOP to begin.

In a small bowl, add the oil and garlic. Stir well to combine.

Once the cauliflower is finished cooking, turn the pressure-release valve to the VENT position. Wait until the pressure has been released, then remove the pressure lid.

Brush the oil-garlic mixture evenly over the cauliflower steaks, then sprinkle the Parmesan cheese over the top.

Close the crisping lid and press AIR CRISP. Set the temperature to 390°F and the time to 10 minutes. Press START/STOP to begin.

When cooking is finished, carefully remove the cauliflower steaks and season to taste with salt. Garnish with the parsley before serving.

CHICKEN TENDERS

SERVES 4

1 CUP ALL-PURPOSE FLOUR

2 EGGS, BEATEN

½ CUP WATER + 2 TABLESPOONS, DIVIDED

2 CUPS ITALIAN BREAD CRUMBS

1 POUND BONELESS, SKINLESS CHICKEN TENDERS

SALT, TO TASTE

In a bowl, add the flour. In another bowl, add the eggs with 2 tablespoons water; mix well. In a third bowl, add the Italian bread crumbs.

Working in batches, dredge each chicken tender into the flour, shaking off the excess. Next, dip into the egg wash, then into the bread crumbs, coating evenly.

Place the reversible rack into the cooking pot, in the higher position. Arrange the chicken tenders on the rack, but do not overlap. Close the crisping lid and select BAKE/ROAST. Set the temperature to 360°F and the time to 12 minutes. Press START/STOP to begin.

When cooking is finished, remove the chicken tenders, and season with salt. Serve immediately with your favorite dipping sauce.

ENGLISH MUFFIN PIZZAS

SERVES 1

1 English muffin, sliced in
  half
¼ cup homemade pizza sauce
  (see below)
8 to 10 slices pepperoni
½ cup low-fat shredded
  mozzarella cheese
1 pinch dried oregano
garlic salt, to taste

Place the reversible rack in the higher position in the cooking pot. Close the crisping lid. Preheat the appliance by selecting BROIL and setting the time to 3 minutes. Select START/STOP to begin.

After 3 minutes, place the English muffin halves on the rack. Close the crisping lid, select BROIL, and set the time to 3 minutes. Select START/STOP to begin.

Remove the English muffin and spread the homemade pizza sauce over each muffin half, followed by equal amounts of pepperoni. Cover with cheese and season each muffin with a little dried oregano and a sprinkle of garlic salt.

Close the crisping lid, select BROIL, and set the time to 3 minutes. Select START/STOP to begin.

When the cheese is melted and bubbly, remove the pizzas from the rack and let cool slightly before serving.

HOMEMADE PIZZA SAUCE

1 (28-ounce) can San Marzano tomato puree (or diced)

2 garlic cloves, peeled and
  rough chopped
½ tablespoon grapeseed oil
1 teaspoon oregano (or
  Italian seasoning)
3–4 fresh basil leaves, torn

In a blender, add the tomatoes, garlic, oil, oregano, and basil. Blend until smooth.

Store in refrigerator until ready to use.

GREEN BEAN FRIES

SERVES 4

2 EGGS

1 POUND FRESH GREEN BEANS,
  WASHED AND DRIED

½ CUP GRATED PARMESAN
  CHEESE

1 TABLESPOON GARLIC SALT

1 CUP PANKO BREAD CRUMBS

In a mixing bowl, whisk together the eggs, then add the green beans.

In a separate bowl, combine the Parmesan cheese, garlic salt, and bread crumbs.

Remove the beans from the egg wash and toss well in the bread crumb mixture.

Place the breaded beans in the cook and crisp basket and place basket in the cooking pot. Close the crisping lid and press AIR CRISP. Set the temperature to 390°F and the time to 5 minutes. Press START/STOP to begin.

After 5 minutes, remove the beans and serve.

HALIBUT FISH AND CHIPS

SERVES 4

1 CUP FLOUR

1 TEASPOON SEA SALT

2 EGGS, BEATEN

2 TABLESPOONS WATER

2 CUPS LOUISIANA FISH FRY
SEASONING

4 (6- TO 8-OUNCE) HALIBUT
(OR COD) FILLETS, CUT INTO
CHUNKS

TARTAR SAUCE

LEMON WEDGES

In a bowl, add the flour and salt. In another bowl, add the eggs whisked with the water. In a third bowl, add the Louisiana Fish Fry seasoning.

Working in batches, dredge each piece of fish into the flour, shaking off the excess. Next, dip into the egg wash, then into the Louisiana Fish Fry seasoning, coating evenly. Keep in refrigerator until ready to cook.

Place the battered fish into the cook and crisp basket and place basket in the cooking pot.

Secure the pressure lid and turn the pressure-release valve to the SEAL position.

Close the crisping lid and press AIR CRISP. Set the temperature to 390°F and the time to 10 minutes. Press START/STOP to begin.

When cooking is finished, remove the fish. Serve immediately with a side of tartar sauce and lemon wedges.

PIEROGI WITH FRESH CHIVES

SERVES 6

2 CUPS WATER

2 POUNDS FROZEN PIEROGI

2 TABLESPOONS GRAPESEED OIL

1 TABLESPOON FRESH CHIVES,
CHOPPED

Pour the water into the cooking pot.

Place the pierogi into the cook and crisp basket and place basket in the pot.

Secure the pressure lid and turn the pressure-release valve to the VENT position.

Select STEAM and set the time to 10 minutes. Press START/STOP to begin.

After 10 minutes, transfer the pierogi to a suitable bowl and toss with the grapeseed oil. Return the pierogi to the basket.

Close the crisping lid and press AIR CRISP. Set the temperature to 375°F and the time to 20 minutes. Press START/STOP to begin.

After 10 minutes, open the lid and remove the basket. Shake the pierogi and then return the basket to the pot to continue cooking.

When cooking is complete, remove the pierogi and serve with a sprinkling of fresh chives.

PRETZEL BITES

SERVES 8

1 PACKAGE PILLSBURY™
CRESCENT ROLLS

2 TABLESPOONS UNSALTED
BUTTER, MELTED

3 TABLESPOONS COARSE SALT

MUSTARD, YOUR PREFERENCE

Unroll the dough per the package directions. Keep the dough in one piece. Using a dough or pizza cutter, cut the dough into long strips. Next, twist each strip of dough into a pretzel or other creative shape.

Brush the pretzels with melted butter and sprinkle with coarse salt.

Place the pretzel in the cook and crisp basket and place the basket in the cooking pot. Close the crisping lid and press AIR CRISP. Set the temperature to 330°F and the time to 5 to 6 minutes, or until the pretzels are golden brown. Press START/STOP to begin.

After cooking, remove the pretzels and let cool before serving with a side of mustard.

PULLED PORK

SERVES 6 TO 8

4 TABLESPOONS BARBECUE
   SAUCE

2 TABLESPOONS GARLIC SALT

1 TABLESPOON SEASONING SALT

1½ CUPS APPLE CIDER VINEGAR

3½ POUNDS BONELESS PORK
   SHOULDER, FAT TRIMMED,
   CUT INTO 1-INCH PIECES

6 OUNCES TOMATO PASTE

Add the barbecue sauce, garlic salt, seasoning salt, and vinegar to the cooking pot. Stir well and then add the pork shoulder.

Secure the pressure lid and turn the pressure-release valve to the SEAL position. Select PRESSURE and set to HIGH. Set the time to 35 minutes. Press START/STOP to begin.

After 35 minutes, turn the pressure-release valve to the VENT position. Wait until the pressure has been released, then remove the pressure lid.

Select SEAR/SAUTÉ and set to MEDIUM-HIGH. Press START/STOP to begin. Note: You will not be using a lid during this step.

Add the tomato paste and stir to incorporate. Allow the pork to simmer for 10 minutes, or until the liquid is reduced, stirring occasionally.

When cooking is finished, remove the pork and, using silicone or scratch-resistant tongs, shred the pork. Serve warm (or use to make Pork Tacos; see page 78).

TURKEY KIELBASA WITH GREEN BEANS AND POTATOES

SERVES 4

1 TABLESPOON GRAPESEED OIL

1 POUND LOW-SODIUM TURKEY KIELBASA SMOKED SAUSAGE

1 POUND FRESH GREEN BEANS, TRIMMED

3 OR 4 POTATOES, CUT INTO CHUNKS

2 CUPS LOW-SODIUM CHICKEN STOCK

Preheat the appliance for 5 minutes by pressing SEAR/SAUTÉ and set to HIGH. Press START/STOP to begin. Note: You will not be using a lid until instructed.

After 5 minutes, add the oil. When hot, add the sausage and brown on both sides. Add the potatoes and chicken stock.

Close the crisping lid, and press BAKE/ROAST. Set the temperature to 400°F and set time to 1½ hours. Press START/STOP to begin. Add the green beans the last 10 minutes of cooking time. Make sure the beans are submerged in the liquid, otherwise they will shrivel and burn.

When cooking is complete, remove the sausage and serve alongside the green beans and potatoes.

Classics, Comforts, and Mains

ALDER PLANK SALMON

SERVES 2

1 SMALL UNTREATED ALDER
    PLANK (7X7), SOAKED IN
    WATER OR WHITE WINE FOR
    AT LEAST 1 HOUR
2 WILD SALMON FILLETS (ABOUT
    6 OUNCES EACH)
1 TEASPOON GRAPESEED OIL
SEASONING SALT, TO TASTE
2 TABLESPOONS LIGHT SOY
    SAUCE
2 TABLESPOONS BROWN SUGAR
1 TEASPOON, FRESH DILL,
    CHOPPED
1 CUP WHITE WINE

Remove the plank from the liquid and place the salmon on the plank, skin-side down. Brush the fillets with a little grapeseed oil and season with the seasoning salt.

In a small bowl, combine the soy sauce and brown sugar. Whisk until the sugar has dissolved. Brush on top of the fillets. Then add the dill to each fillet.

Pour the wine in the cooking pot. Place the plank on the reversible rack and place in the pot in the higher position.

Secure the pressure lid and turn the pressure-release valve to the SEAL position.

Select PRESSURE and set to HIGH. Set the time to 4 minutes. Press START/STOP to begin.

After 4 minutes, turn the pressure-release valve to the VENT position. Wait until the pressure has been released, then remove the pressure lid.

Close the crisping lid. Select AIR CRISP and set the temperature to 400°F and the time to 5 minutes. Check the doneness before removing from rack. Cook an additional 1 to 2 minutes if need be.

Serve the salmon on the alder plank.

ASIAN CHICKEN BREASTS WITH CAULIFLOWER AND WILD RICE

SERVES 2

1 CUP WILD RICE, RINSED

1 CUP LOW-SODIUM CHICKEN
STOCK

2 TEASPOONS SALT, DIVIDED

2 TEASPOONS FRESH GROUND
BLACK PEPPER, DIVIDED

2 (8 OUNCES EACH) FRESH
BONELESS CHICKEN BREASTS

1 HEAD CAULIFLOWER, CUT
INTO SMALL FLORETS

1 TABLESPOON GRAPESEED OIL

¼ CUP TERIYAKI SAUCE

Place the wild rice, chicken stock, 1 teaspoon salt, and 1 teaspoon black pepper in the cooking pot. Stir to combine.

Place the chicken breasts on the reversible rack and place the rack in the pot in the higher position, above the rice.

Secure the pressure lid and turn the pressure-release valve to the SEAL position.

Select PRESSURE and set to HIGH. Set the time to 2 minutes. Press START/STOP to begin.

In a medium-sized bowl, toss the cauliflower florets with the grapeseed oil. Season with the remaining salt and pepper.

After 2 minutes, allow the pressure to naturally release for 10 minutes. Then, switch the valve to the VENT position. Wait until the pressure has been released, then remove the pressure lid.

Brush the chicken breasts with the teriyaki sauce and add the cauliflower to the rack around the chicken.

Close the crisping lid and press BROIL. Set the time to 18 minutes. Press START/STOP to begin.

Cooking is finished when the internal temperature of the chicken reaches 165°F. Use a kitchen thermometer to check.

Remove the chicken, cauliflower, and rice, and serve immediately.

BEEF AND BARLEY SOUP

SERVES 6

1 TABLESPOON VEGETABLE OIL

2½ POUNDS LEAN BEEF STEW
    MEAT, CUT INTO 1-INCH
    PIECES

1 YELLOW ONION, PEELED AND
    FINELY CHOPPED

4 STALKS CELERY, FINELY
    CHOPPED

4 CARROTS, PEELED AND FINELY
    CHOPPED

2 SPRIGS FRESH OREGANO

½ TEASPOON SALT

¼ TEASPOON FRESH CRACKED
    BLACK PEPPER

2 TABLESPOONS TOMATO PASTE

14½ OUNCES SAN MARZANO
    DICED TOMATOES

6 CUPS LOW-SODIUM BEEF
    STOCK

1 CUP PEARL BARLEY

Preheat the appliance for 5 minutes by pressing SEAR/SAUTÉ and set to HIGH. Press START/STOP to begin. Note: You will not be using a lid until instructed.

After 5 minutes, add the oil and then the beef in batches. Brown the meat on all sides, then remove and set aside. Add the onion, celery, carrots, oregano, salt, and pepper. Cook for 5 minutes. Add the tomato paste, diced tomatoes, beef stock, barley, and the browned beef. Press START/STOP to turn off appliance.

Secure the pressure lid and turn the pressure-release valve to the SEAL position.

Select PRESSURE and set to HIGH. Set the time to 22 minutes. Press START/STOP to begin.

After 22 minutes, allow the pressure to naturally release for 10 minutes. Then, switch the valve to the VENT position. Wait until the pressure has been released, then remove the pressure lid.

Serve the soup immediately.

CHEESY BAKED PENNE

SERVES 6

5 CUPS WATER

16 OUNCES DRIED PENNE PASTA

1 CUP HEAVY CREAM

16 OUNCES SHREDDED
BEECHER'S FLAGSHIP
CHEESE (OR LOW-FAT ROBUST
CHEDDAR)

1 TABLESPOONS SALT

1 TABLESPOON FRESH GROUND
BLACK PEPPER

1 TABLESPOON GARLIC SALT

1 TABLESPOON ONION POWDER

2 CUPS ITALIAN BREAD CRUMBS

½ CUP UNSALTED BUTTER,
MELTED

Add the water and dry pasta to the cooking pot.

Secure the pressure lid and turn the pressure-release valve to the SEAL position. Select PRESSURE and set to LOW. Set the time to 1 minute. Press START/STOP to begin.

After 1 minute, allow the pressure to naturally release for 10 minutes. Then, switch the valve to the VENT position. Wait until the pressure has been released, then remove the pressure lid.

Add the cream, cheese, salt, pepper, garlic salt, and onion powder to the pot. Stir until well incorporated into the pasta.

In a small bowl, add the bread crumbs and melted butter. Stir well to combine and add to the pasta, to cover.

Close the crisping lid and press AIR CRISP. Set the temperature to 360°F and the time to 7 minutes. Press START/STOP to begin.

Cooking is finished when the bread crumb mixture is golden brown. Serve immediately.

CHICKEN AND DUMPLINGS

SERVES 6

2 TABLESPOONS GRAPESEED OIL

1 YELLOW ONION, PEELED AND FINELY CHOPPED

3 STALKS CELERY, FINELY CHOPPED

2 CARROTS, PEELED AND FINELY CHOPPED

2 GARLIC CLOVES, PEELED AND MINCED

2 SPRIGS FRESH THYME

2 SHORT SPRIGS FRESH ROSEMARY

1½ TEASPOONS SALT

½ TEASPOON FRESH CRACKED BLACK PEPPER

2 POUNDS BONELESS SKINLESS CHICKEN BREASTS

6 CUPS LOW-SODIUM CHICKEN STOCK

10½ OUNCES CREAM OF CHICKEN SOUP

1½ CUPS CARBQUIK™ COMPLETE BISCUIT AND BAKING MIX

½ CUP LOW-FAT MILK

1 BUNCH FRESH ITALIAN FLAT-LEAF PARSLEY, FINELY CHOPPED

Close the crisping lid. Preheat the appliance for 5 minutes by pressing SEAR/SAUTÉ and set to MEDIUM-HIGH. Press START/STOP to begin.

After 5 minutes, open the lid and add the oil, onion, celery, and carrots. Stir occasionally. Add the garlic, thyme, rosemary, salt, and pepper. Cook for 2 minutes, uncovered, while continuing to stir occasionally. Add the chicken, stock, and cream of chicken soup. Stir well.

Secure the pressure lid and turn the pressure-release valve to the SEAL position.

Select PRESSURE and set to HIGH. Set the time to 15 minutes. Press START/STOP to begin.

In a mixing bowl, add the Carbquik and milk. Mix well until dough forms, then shape into small 1-inch dough balls.

When cooking is complete, turn the pressure-release valve to the VENT position. Wait until the pressure has been released, then remove the pressure lid.

Transfer the chicken to a bowl and shred into small pieces. Return the chicken to the pot.

Close the crisping lid. Press SEAR/SAUTÉ and set to MEDIUM-HIGH. Press START/STOP to begin. When the liquid begins to simmer, drop the dough balls into the pot. Cook for 10 minutes.

After 10 minutes, press START/STOP to turn off the appliance. Keep the crisping lid closed and let the contents rest for 5 minutes before removing from the pot and serving with fresh parsley on top.

CHICKEN, LEEK, AND WILD RICE SOUP

SERVES 6

4 CARROTS, PEELED AND FINELY
CHOPPED

4 STALKS CELERY, TRIMMED AND
FINELY CHOPPED

2 LEEKS, TRIMMED, CUT IN HALF
LENGTHWISE, THINLY SLICED

½ CUP WILD RICE, RINSED

2 SPRIGS FRESH THYME

4 CUPS LOW-SODIUM CHICKEN
STOCK, DIVIDED

1½ POUNDS BONELESS, SKINLESS
CHICKEN BREASTS, CUT INTO
STRIPS

1½ TEASPOONS SALT

1½ TEASPOONS FRESH CRACKED
BLACK PEPPER

1 CUP WATER

Add the carrots, celery, leeks, wild rice, thyme, and 1½ cups of chicken stock in the cooking pot. Add the chicken on top and season with the salt and pepper.

Secure the pressure lid and turn the pressure-release valve to the SEAL position.

Select PRESSURE and set to HIGH. Set the time to 2 minutes. Press START/STOP to begin.

After 2 minutes, allow the pressure to naturally release for 10 minutes. Then, switch the valve to the VENT position. Wait until the pressure has been released, then remove the pressure lid.

Add the remaining chicken stock and the water. Close the pressure lid. Select SEAR/SAUTÉ and set to HIGH. Press START/STOP to begin and let simmer for 5 minutes. Note: You may need to add additional liquid to achieve a soup-like consistency.

When cooking is complete, transfer to serving bowls and serve immediately.

CHICKEN TORTILLA SOUP

SERVES 8

1 TABLESPOON VEGETABLE OIL

1¼ POUNDS BONELESS, SKINLESS
CHICKEN BREASTS, HALVED

1 YELLOW ONION, PEELED AND
DICED

2 GARLIC CLOVES, PEELED AND
MINCED

¼ CUP FRESH CILANTRO, FINELY
CHOPPED

14½ OUNCES SAN MARZANO
DICED TOMATOES, DRAINED

20 OUNCES ENCHILADA SAUCE

14½ OUNCES LOW-SODIUM
CHICKEN STOCK

15 OUNCES BLACK BEANS, WITH
LIQUID

10 OUNCES CORN

1 TABLESPOON CHILI POWDER

1 TABLESPOON CUMIN

5 SMALL CORN TORTILLAS, CUT
INTO STRIPS

1 AVOCADO, PITTED, PEELED,
AND SLICED, FOR GARNISH

Add the oil to the cooking pot. Select SEAR/SAUTÉ and set to MEDIUM. Press START/STOP to begin and heat oil. When oil is hot, add the chicken. Cook uncovered until chicken is lightly brown on each side, about 5 minutes.

Add the onion, garlic, cilantro, diced tomatoes, enchilada sauce, chicken stock, black beans with liquid, corn, chili, powder, and cumin.

Secure the pressure lid and turn the pressure-release valve to the SEAL position.

Select SLOW COOK and set to HIGH. Set the time for 2 to 3 hours. Press START/STOP to begin.

When cooking is complete, shred the chicken while it is in the pot. Then serve into individual bowls topped with the tortilla strips and avocado slices.

CORN BREAD

SERVES 6 TO 8

1¼ CUPS FLOUR

¾ CUP CORNMEAL

2 TEASPOONS BAKING POWDER

¼ CUP SUGAR

2 TEASPOONS SALT

1 EGG

2 CUPS LOW-FAT MILK

¼ CUP VEGETABLE OIL

Place the reversible rack in the cooking pot, in the lower position. Place a greased multipurpose 8-inch baking pan on top of the rack. Close the crisping lid, preheat the appliance by pressing BROIL, and set the time to 10 minutes. Press START/STOP to begin.

In a mixing bowl, add the flour, cornmeal, baking powder, sugar, and salt. Whisk well until combined. Add the egg, milk, and oil and whisk together until a batter consistency is achieved.

Open the crisping lid and pour the corn bread batter into the greased baking pan.

Close the crisping lid. Press BAKE/ROAST and set the temperature to 350°F for 20 minutes. Press START/STOP to begin.

Cooking is complete when the corn bread is golden brown and a toothpick inserted into the center comes out clean. If the corn bread is not done after 20 minutes, cook for an additional 5 minutes.

Remove from the pan and serve warm.

CRISPY RABBIT
WITH CARROTS AND WILD RICE

SERVES 4

6 OUNCES WILD RICE, RINSED

1¾ CUP LOW-SODIUM
VEGETABLE STOCK

1 TABLESPOON UNSALTED
BUTTER

1 RABBIT, CUT INTO 8 PIECES

4 CARROTS, PEELED AND CUT IN
HALF LENGTHWISE

2 TABLESPOONS AGAVE NECTAR

½ TEASPOON SMOKED PAPRIKA

½ TEASPOON GROUND CUMIN

2 TEASPOONS SALT, DIVIDED

1 TABLESPOON GRAPESEED OIL

Add the rice, vegetable stock, and butter to the cooking pot. Stir well.

Place the reversible rack into the pot, in the higher position, above the rice mixture. Add the rabbit along with the carrots.

Secure the pressure lid and turn the pressure-release valve to the SEAL position. Select PRESSURE and set to HIGH. Set the time to 4 minutes. Press START/STOP to begin.

In a small bowl, add the agave nectar, smoked paprika, cumin, and 1 teaspoon salt.

After 4 minutes, turn the pressure-release valve to the VENT position. Wait until the pressure has been released, then remove the pressure lid.

Brush the carrots with the agave-spice mixture and brush the rabbit with the grapeseed oil. Sprinkle the remaining teaspoon of salt over the rabbit and carrots.

Close the crisping lid, press BROIL, and set the time to 10 minutes. Press START/STOP to begin.

When cooking is finished (internal temperature 160°F), remove the rabbit, carrots and rice, and serve immediately.

COUNTRY CHICKEN

SERVES 4 TO 6

1 WHOLE CHICKEN (5–7
POUNDS)

1 LEMON, JUICED

1 ORANGE, JUICED

1 LIME, JUICED

¼ CUP LOW-SODIUM CHICKEN
STOCK

1 TABLESPOON BLACK
PEPPERCORNS

5 SPRIGS FRESH THYME

5 OR 6 CLOVES GARLIC, PEELED
AND CRUSHED

1 TABLESPOON GRAPESEED OIL

2 TABLESPOONS UNSALTED
BUTTER, MELTED

SALT AND PEPPER, TO TASTE

Rinse the chicken under cold water and pat dry with paper towel. Remove the giblets, if included.

In a small bowl, add the lemon juice, orange juice, lime juice, chicken stock, and black pepper. Mix well and add to the cooking pot. Next, add the peppercorns, thyme, and garlic.

Place the chicken into the cook and crisp basket and place the basket in the pot.

Secure the pressure lid and turn the pressure-release valve to the SEAL position. Select PRESSURE and set to HIGH. Set the time to 20 minutes. Press START/STOP to begin.

After 20 minutes, turn the pressure-release valve to the VENT position. Wait until the pressure has been released, then remove the pressure lid.

Brush the chicken with the oil and butter and season with salt and pepper.

Close the crisping lid and press AIR CRISP. Set the temperature to 400°F and the time to 30 minutes. Press START/STOP to begin.

Cooking is finished when the chicken is golden brown and the internal temperature of the chicken reaches 165°F. Use a kitchen thermometer to check.

Remove the chicken from the cook and crisp basket and let it rest for 5 to 10 minutes before serving.

COUNTRY POTATOES

SERVES 4

½ CUP WATER

4 RUSSET POTATOES, CUT INTO
WEDGES

2 TABLESPOONS GRAPESEED OIL,
DIVIDED

1 TABLESPOON FRESH ITALIAN
FLAT-LEAF PARSLEY, MINCED

4 GARLIC CLOVES, PEELED AND
MINCED

2 TEASPOONS SALT

1 TEASPOON FRESH GROUND
BLACK PEPPER

Pour the water into the cooking pot.

Carefully place the potato wedges into the cook and crisp basket and place the basket in the pot.

Secure the pressure lid and turn the pressure-release valve to the SEAL position. Select PRESSURE and set to LOW. Set the time to 3 minutes. Press START/STOP to begin.

In a small bowl, add 1 tablespoon of the grapeseed oil, parsley, garlic, salt, and pepper. Mix well to combine. Set aside.

After 3 minutes, turn the pressure-release valve to the VENT position. Wait until the pressure has been released, then remove the pressure lid. Drizzle the remaining tablespoon of grapeseed oil over the potatoes.

Close the crisping lid and press AIR CRISP. Set the temperature to 400°F and the time to 18 minutes. Press START/STOP to begin. Check the potatoes after 12 minutes. Continue cooking if the potatoes are undercooked.

When cooking is finished, remove the potato wedges and toss in the oil-parsley mixture before serving.

FAMILY-STYLE POT ROAST WITH VEGETABLES AND GRAVY

SERVES 4 TO 6

3½ POUNDS LEAN BONELESS CHUCK ROAST

LAWRY'S® SEASONED SALT

¼ CUP ALL-PURPOSE FLOUR

1 TABLESPOON GRAPESEED OIL

1 LARGE YELLOW ONION, PEELED AND CHOPPED

3 GARLIC CLOVES, PEELED AND SMASHED

1 TABLESPOON TOMATO PASTE

½ CUP RED WINE

1½ CUPS LOW-SODIUM BEEF STOCK

1 SPRIG FRESH THYME

1 BAY LEAF

4 CARROTS, PEELED AND SLICED INTO 2-INCH PIECES ON THE BIAS

2 LARGE RUSSET POTATOES, PEELED AND QUARTERED

2 TABLESPOONS CORNSTARCH

2 TABLESPOONS WATER

Preheat the appliance for 5 minutes by selecting SEAR/SAUTÉ and setting to HIGH. Press START/STOP to begin. Note: You will not be using a lid until instructed.

Season the roast with the seasoning salt, then coat in the flour.

After 5 minutes, add the oil to the cooking pot. When the oil is hot, add the roast. Allow the roast to brown on all sides. Remove the roast and set aside.

Add the onion, garlic, and tomato paste to the pot. Cook for 3 minutes. Add the wine, beef stock, thyme, bay leaf, carrots, and potatoes.

Secure the pressure lid and turn the pressure-release valve to the SEAL position.

Select PRESSURE and set to HIGH. Set the time to 50 minutes. Press START/STOP to begin.

After 50 minutes, allow the pressure to naturally release for 30 minutes. After 30 minutes, switch the valve to the VENT position. Wait until the pressure has been released, then remove the pressure lid.

Remove the roast and vegetables from the pot and keep warm. Remove the thyme and bay leaf from the pot and discard.

In a small bowl, add the cornstarch and water and stir until the cornstarch has dissolved.

Select SEAR/SAUTÉ and set to MEDIUM-HIGH. Select START/STOP to begin. Bring the liquid to a simmer, uncovered, then add the cornstarch-water mixture. Stir until a gravy-like consistency is achieved.

Serve with roast and vegetables alongside the gravy.

HAWAIIAN FRIED RICE

SERVES 4 TO 6

1 CUP JASMINE RICE, RINSED

1 CUP WATER

2 TABLESPOONS SESAME OIL,
   DIVIDED

¼ CUP GREEN PEAS

⅓ CUP CELERY, DICED

⅓ CUP CARROTS, PEELED AND
   DICED

½ CUP PINEAPPLE CHUNKS,
   DICED

½ CUP COOKED LOW-SODIUM
   HAM, DICED

1 TEASPOON FRESH GINGER,
   GRATED

2 TEASPOONS TAMARI

2 EGGS, BEATEN

2 SCALLIONS, THINLY SLICED ON
   THE BIAS

SALT, TO TASTE

Add the rice, water, and sesame oil to the cooking pot.

Secure the pressure lid and turn the pressure-release valve to the SEAL position. Select PRESSURE and set to HIGH. Set the time to 1 minute. Press START/STOP to begin.

After 1 minute, switch the valve to the VENT position. Wait until the pressure has been released, then remove the pressure lid. Add the peas, celery, carrots, pineapple, ham, ginger, and tamari. Stir well to combine.

Close the crisping lid and press AIR CRISP. Set the temperature to 390°F and the time to 10 minutes. Press START/STOP to begin.

After 10 minutes, open the lid. Make a well in the center of the rice and pour in the eggs. Press SEAR/SAUTÉ on HIGH. Press START/STOP to begin. Cook while continuing to stir until the eggs are scrambled and incorporated into the rice. Add the sliced scallions and season to taste with salt just before serving.

ITALIAN SAUSAGE AND PEPPER HOAGIES

SERVES 6

1 TABLESPOON GRAPESEED OIL

6 ITALIAN SAUSAGES (SWEET, MILD, OR HOT)

1 CUP RED BELL PEPPER, SLICED

1 CUP YELLOW BELL PEPPER, SLICED

1 CUP SWEET YELLOW ONIONS, PEELED AND SLICED

28 OUNCES SAN MARZANO CRUSHED TOMATOES

½ CUP WATER

1½ TEASPOONS ITALIAN SEASONING

6 FRESH HOAGIE ROLLS, WARMED OR TOASTED

12 SLICES LOW-FAT MOZZARELLA CHEESE (OPTIONAL)

Add the grapeseed oil to the cooking pot.

Select SEAR/SAUTÉ and set to HIGH. Press START/STOP to begin. Note: You will not be using a lid until instructed. When the oil is hot, add the sausages, bell peppers, and onions. Cook until the sausage is cooked through and the vegetables are soft. Press START/STOP to turn off appliance.

Add the crushed tomatoes, water, and Italian seasoning. Stir well to combine.

Secure the pressure lid and turn the pressure-release valve to the SEAL position. Select SEAR/SAUTÉ and set to HIGH for 20 minutes. Press START/STOP to begin.

After 20 minutes, allow the pressure to naturally release, then switch the valve to the VENT position. Wait until the pressure has been released, then remove the pressure lid.

Stir again and fill the hoagie rolls with the sausage and peppers. Top each hoagie with two sliced of mozzarella cheese, if desired, and serve.

JAMBALAYA

SERVES 6

2 TABLESPOONS GRAPESEED OIL

3 ANDOUILLE SAUSAGE, SLICED
INTO ROUNDS

1 POUND BONELESS SKINLESS
CHICKEN BREASTS, CUT INTO
1-INCH PIECES

1 TABLESPOON CAJUN
SEASONING

1 GREEN BELL PEPPER, SEEDED
AND DICED

1 ONION, PEELED AND DICED

2 STALKS CELERY

3 CLOVES GARLIC, PEELED AND
MINCED

½ TEASPOON RED PEPPER
FLAKES

1 TEASPOON GARLIC SALT

½ TEASPOON FRESH CRACKED
BLACK PEPPER

2 TEASPOONS WORCESTERSHIRE
SAUCE

1 TEASPOON FILÉ POWDER

16 OUNCES SAN MARZANO
DICED TOMATOES

1¼ CUPS WHITE LONG-GRAIN
RICE

2½ CUPS LOW-SODIUM CHICKEN
STOCK

Add the oil, sausage, chicken, and Cajun seasoning to the cooking pot. Stir well to combine. Note: You will not be using a lid until instructed.

Select SEAR/SAUTÉ and set to HIGH. Press START/STOP to begin. Cook until the sausage and chicken are browned and cooked through. Remove from the pot and add the bell pepper, onion, celery, and garlic. Sauté until vegetables are softened. Add the red pepper flakes, garlic salt, black pepper, Worcestershire sauce, filé powder, and tomatoes. Return the sausage and chicken to the pot. Add the rice and chicken stock and stir all the ingredients well until combined. Press START/STOP to turn off appliance.

Secure the pressure lid and turn the pressure-release valve to the SEAL position. Select SEAR/SAUTÉ and set to HIGH for 12 minutes. Press START/STOP to begin.

When cooking is complete, turn the pressure-release valve to the VENT position. Wait until the pressure has been released, then remove the pressure lid.

Stir well and serve immediately.

LOBSTER COUSCOUS

SERVES 4 TO 6

¼ CUP + 1 TABLESPOON
UNSALTED BUTTER, DIVIDED

2 SHALLOTS, PEELED AND DICED

1 TABLESPOON GARLIC, PEELED
AND DICED

¾ CUP WHITE WINE

1 POUND FRESH OR FROZEN
LOBSTER TAIL MEAT,
SHELLED AND CHOPPED

½ CUP LOW-SODIUM CHICKEN
STOCK

1 TABLESPOON LEMON JUICE

¼ TEASPOON RED PEPPER
FLAKES

SALT AND FRESH CRACKED
BLACK PEPPER, TO TASTE

1 CUP COUSCOUS

¼ CUP GRATED PARMESAN
CHEESE

2 TABLESPOONS FRESH ITALIAN
FLAT-LEAF PARSLEY, FINELY
CHOPPED

Preheat the appliance for 5 minutes by pressing SEAR/SAUTÉ and set to MEDIUM-HIGH. Press START/STOP to begin. Note: You will not be using a lid until instructed.

After 5 minutes, add ¼ cup of butter to the cooking pot. When the butter has melted, add the shallots and garlic, and cook for 1 minute while stirring. Add the wine, and cook until liquid is reduced, about 1 minute. Add the lobster meat, chicken stock, lemon juice, and red pepper flakes. Stir well and season to taste with salt and pepper.

Secure the pressure lid and turn the pressure-release valve to the SEAL position. Select PRESSURE and set to HIGH. Set time to 1 minute. Press START/STOP to begin.

After 1 minute, turn the pressure-release valve to the VENT position. Wait until the pressure has been released, then remove the pressure lid.

Add the couscous and the remaining tablespoon of butter. Stir to combine, then cover and let sit for 5 minutes.

After 5 minutes, add the Parmesan cheese and parsley. Stir well and serve immediately.

MAC AND CHEESE

SERVES 6

½ CUP MARGARINE

1 ONION, PEELED AND FINELY
   CHOPPED

¼ CUP FLOUR

1 TEASPOON SALT

1 TEASPOON FRESH CRACKED
   BLACK PEPPER

2½ CUPS LOW-FAT MILK

1 TABLESPOON MUSTARD

½ TABLESPOON
   WORCESTERSHIRE SAUCE

2½ CUPS ELBOW MACARONI

2 CUPS SHREDDED LOW-FAT
   CHEDDAR CHEESE

FRESH DILL, FOR GARNISH

Add the margarine and onion to the cooking pot.

Select SEAR/SAUTE and set to HIGH for 10 minutes. Press START/STOP to begin. Note: You will not be using a lid until instructed.

Cook the onions, stirring often, until soft. Whisk in the flour, salt, pepper, milk, mustard, and Worcestershire sauce. Add the macaroni and stir well to combine.

Secure the pressure lid and turn the pressure release valve to the SEAL position. Select PRESSURE and set to HIGH. Set time to 3 minutes. Press START/STOP to begin.

After 3 minutes, allow the pressure to naturally release for 1 minute 30 seconds, then switch the valve to the VENT position. Wait until the pressure has been released, then remove the pressure lid.

Add the cheddar cheese. Stir well, remove from pot, and garnish with some fresh dill before serving.

MISO-GLAZED STEELHEAD WITH JASMINE RICE AND CHINESE BROCCOLI

SERVES 4

1 CUP JASMINE RICE, RINSED

¾ CUP LOW-SODIUM VEGETABLE STOCK

1 TEASPOON SALT

2 TABLESPOONS RED MISO PASTE

2 TABLESPOONS UNSALTED BUTTER, SOFTENED

1 BUNCH CHINESE BROCCOLI

1 TEASPOON SESAME OIL

¼ CUP MIRIN

4 (4 OUNCES EACH) SKINLESS STEELHEAD FILLETS

Place the rice and vegetable stock into the cooking pot. Stir to combine.

Secure the pressure lid and turn the pressure-release valve to the SEAL position. Select PRESSURE and set to HIGH. Set the time to 2 minutes. Press START/STOP to begin.

In a small bowl, add the red miso paste and butter. Mix well to form a paste.

Toss the Chinese broccoli with the sesame oil and mirin.

After 2 minutes, turn the pressure-release valve to the VENT position. Wait until the pressure has been released, then remove the pressure lid.

Gently pat the steelhead fillets with paper towels. Season with salt, spread the miso paste on top of each fillet, and place in the reversible rack. Place the rack in the pot, in the higher position, above the rice. Add the Chinese broccoli to the rack, around the steelhead.

Close the crisping lid and press BROIL. Set the time to 12 minutes. Press START/STOP to begin.

Cooking is finished when the internal temperature of the fish reaches 145°F. Use a kitchen thermometer to check.

Remove the steelhead, Chinese broccoli, and rice, and serve immediately.

PANKO-CRUSTED HALIBUT WITH BABY BOK CHOY AND WILD RICE

SERVES 4

1 CUP BASMATI WHITE RICE, RINSED

1 CUP LOW-SODIUM CHICKEN STOCK

1 CUP PANKO BREAD CRUMBS

¼ CUP UNSALTED BUTTER, MELTED

¼ CUP MINCED FRESH ITALIAN FLAT-LEAF PARSLEY

2 LEMONS, JUICED AND ZESTED

2 TEASPOONS SEA SALT, DIVIDED

4 (5–6 OUNCES EACH) FRESH HALIBUT FILLETS, SKIN REMOVED

2 BABY BOK CHOY, CUT IN HALF LENGTHWISE

1 TEASPOON GRAPESEED OIL

Place the white rice and chicken stock into the cooking pot. Stir to combine.

Secure the pressure lid and turn the pressure-release valve to the SEAL position. Select PRESSURE and set to HIGH. Set the time to 3 minutes. Press START/STOP to begin.

In a medium-sized bowl, add the bread crumbs, melted butter, parsley, lemon juice, lemon zest, and 1 teaspoon sea salt. Mix well. Top each halibut fillet with the bread crumb mixture.

Once the rice is finished cooking, turn the pressure-release valve to the VENT position. Wait until the pressure has been released, then remove the pressure lid.

Drizzle the bok choy with the oil, and season with the remaining teaspoon of sea salt. Place on top of the rice.

Add the reversible rack in the pot, in the higher position, above the rice and bok choy, and add the halibut fillets, bread crumb–side up.

Close the crisping lid and press BAKE/ROAST. Set the temperature to 350°F and the time to 14 minutes. Press START/STOP to begin.

Cooking is finished when the internal temperature of the fish reaches 145°F. Use a kitchen thermometer to check.

Remove the halibut, bok choy, and rice, and serve immediately.

PORK TACOS

SERVES 12

¾ CUP LOW-SODIUM VEGETABLE
  STOCK

8 GARLIC CLOVES, PEELED AND
  CRUSHED

1 ORANGE, JUICED AND ZESTED

20 LEAVES FRESH OREGANO

2 TEASPOONS CHILI POWDER

1 TABLESPOON SALT

2 TEASPOONS FRESH CRACKED
  BLACK PEPPER

3 POUNDS BONELESS PORK
  SHOULDER, CUT INTO 1-INCH
  PIECES

3 TABLESPOONS HONEY

2 TABLESPOONS FRESH
  CILANTRO, CHOPPED

CORN OR FLOUR TORTILLAS OR
  TACO SHELLS, AS NEEDED

Add the vegetable stock, garlic, orange juice and zest, oregano, chili powder, salt, and pepper into the cooking pot. Stir well and then add the pork shoulder.

Secure the pressure lid and turn the pressure-release valve to the SEAL position. Select PRESSURE and set to HIGH. Set the time to 20 minutes. Press START/STOP to begin.

After 20 minutes, turn the pressure-release valve to the VENT position. Wait until the pressure has been released, then remove the pressure lid.

Remove the pork and shred with a fork. Return the shredded pork to the pot.

Select SEAR/SAUTÉ and set to MEDIUM-HIGH. Allow the pork to simmer, uncovered, for 10 minutes, or until the liquid is reduced, stirring occasionally. Stir the honey into the pork and liquid.

Close the crisping lid, press BROIL, and set the time to 8 minutes. Press START/STOP to begin.

When cooking is finished, open the lid and stir in the cilantro and season if necessary. Serve the shredded pork with warm tortillas and/or taco shells. Top with your favorite toppings, such as sliced avocado, salsa, chopped tomatoes and onion, low-fat sour cream, hot sauce, and lime wedges.

RIB EYE WITH MASHED RED POTATOES AND ASPARAGUS

SERVES 4

5 OR 6 LARGE RED POTATOES,
   CUT IN ½-INCH PIECES

½ CUP WATER

¼ CUP UNSALTED BUTTER

½ CUP HEAVY CREAM

SALT, TO TASTE

FRESH CRACKED BLACK PEPPER,
   TO TASTE

4 (12 OUNCES EACH) RIB EYE
   STEAKS

1 BUNCH ASPARAGUS, ENDS
   TRIMMED

1 TABLESPOON GRAPESEED OIL

Add the potatoes and water to the cooking pot.

Secure the pressure lid and turn the pressure-release valve to the SEAL position. Select PRESSURE and set to HIGH. Set the time to 1 minute. Press START/STOP to begin.

After 1 minute, turn the pressure-release valve to the VENT position. Wait until the pressure has been released, then remove the pressure lid.

Add the butter and cream to the pot with the potatoes. Using a soft kitchen utensil that won't scratch the pot, mash the potatoes until smooth and creamy. Season with salt and pepper.

Place the reversible rack in the pot, in the higher position, over the mashed potatoes. Season the steaks with salt and pepper and arrange on the rack. Toss the asparagus with the oil, season with salt and pepper, and add the asparagus spears to the rack next to the steaks.

Close the crisping lid, press BROIL, and set the time to 5 minutes. Press START/STOP to begin.

After 5 minutes, flip the steaks and continue to broil for another 5 minutes, or until desired doneness, or until the internal temperature of the meat reaches at least 130°F.

When cooking is finished, remove the steaks from the rack and allow to rest for 5 minutes. Serve with the asparagus and mashed potatoes.

SHRIMP WITH WILD RICE

SERVES 4

¼ CUP UNSALTED BUTTER

2 CLOVES GARLIC, PEELED

½ TEASPOON SEA SALT

½ TEASPOON FRESH CRACKED
   BLACK PEPPER

1 TABLESPOON WHITE WINE

1 POUND SHRIMP, PEELED AND
   DEVEINED

¾ CUP LOW-SODIUM VEGETABLE
   STOCK

1 CUP WILD RICE, RINSED

Add the butter, garlic, salt, pepper, and white wine to the cooking pot.

Select SEAR/SAUTE and set to HIGH for 5 minutes. Press START/
STOP to begin. Note: You will not be using a lid until instructed.

Cook, stirring often, until the butter is melted and the garlic is soft.
Add the shrimp and cook until just cooked through. Remove the
shrimp from the pot and set aside.

Add the vegetable stock and wild rice to the pot.

Secure the pressure lid and turn the pressure release valve to the
SEAL position.

Select PRESSURE and set to HIGH. Set the time to 2 minutes. Press
START/STOP to begin.

After 2 minutes, allow the pressure to naturally release for 10 minutes.
Then, switch the valve to the VENT position. Wait until the pressure
has been released, then remove the pressure lid.

Remove the rice and transfer to serving dishes. Return the shrimp to
the pot and stir well with any remaining juices. Remove the shrimp
and serve atop the wild rice.

SPICED CHICKEN WITH CHIMICHURRI

SERVES 2

2 TEASPOONS SALT

1 TABLESPOON SMOKED
    PAPRIKA

1 TABLESPOON CHILI POWDER

1 TABLESPOON GROUND FENNEL

1 TEASPOON FRESH CRACKED
    BLACK PEPPER

1 TEASPOON ONION POWDER

1 TEASPOON GARLIC SALT

1 TEASPOON CUMIN

2 LARGE CHICKEN BREASTS,
    SKIN ON

1 TABLESPOON VEGETABLE OIL

CHIMICHURRI (SEE BELOW)

In a small mixing bowl, add the salt, paprika, chili powder, fennel, pepper, onion powder, garlic salt, and cumin. Mix well to combine. Next, pat the chicken breasts dry and coat with the vegetable oil. Season all sides with the spice mixture.

Preheat the appliance by pressing AIR CRISP and set the temperature to 375°F and the time to 5 minutes. Press START/STOP to begin.

After 5 minutes, add the seasoned chicken to the cook and crisp basket. Close the crisping lid. Select AIR CRISP and set the temperature to 375°F and the time to 25 minutes. Press START/STOP to begin.

After 20 minutes, open the lid and check the chicken to make sure it is cooked through. Cooking is finished when the internal temperature of the chicken is 165°F. Use a kitchen thermometer to check. You may need to cook 5 additional minutes, for a total of 25 minutes cooking time. When cooked, remove the chicken and let rest for 5 minutes before serving with the chimichurri.

CHIMICHURRI

¾ CUP GRAPESEED OIL

½ CUP RED WINE VINEGAR

¼ CUP FRESH ITALIAN FLAT-LEAF PARSLEY,
    MINCED

½ CUP FRESH CILANTRO, MINCED

1 SHALLOT, PEELED AND FINELY CHOPPED

3–4 GARLIC CLOVES, PEELED AND MINCED

1 TEASPOON SALT

In a small mixing bowl, add the oil, vinegar, parsley, cilantro, shallot, garlic, and salt. Whisk until smooth.

STUFFED PEPPERS

SERVES 8

4 LARGE BELL PEPPERS (GREEN
    OR RED)

1 TABLESPOON GARLIC SALT

1 TEASPOON FRESH CRACKED
    BLACK PEPPER

3 TABLESPOONS SMOKED
    PAPRIKA

1 POUND GROUND TURKEY
    (OR BEEF)

1 SMALL ONION, PEELED AND
    MINCED

1 CUP WILD RICE OR BROWN
    RICE, RINSED

1 CUP LOW-SODIUM CHICKEN
    STOCK

½ CUP FRESH ITALIAN FLAT-
    LEAF PARSLEY, CHOPPED

LOW-FAT CHEDDAR CHEESE,
    AS NEEDED

Cut the tops off the peppers, chop up the tops, and set aside. Remove the seeds and stems from the peppers. Cut each in half, lengthwise.

In a mixing bowl, add the garlic salt, pepper, and paprika. Mix well to combine and set aside.

Add the meat, onion, rice, chicken stock, and spice mixture to the cooking pot, breaking apart the meat. Stir well and taste. Adjust if necessary.

Secure the pressure lid and turn the pressure-release valve to the SEAL position. Select PRESSURE and set to HIGH. Set the time to 15 minutes. Press START/STOP to begin.

After 15 minutes, allow the pressure to naturally release for 10 minutes. Then, switch the valve to the VENT position. Wait until the pressure has been released, then remove the pressure lid.

Stir the meat mixture, then add the chopped pepper tops and parsley. Add additional salt if necessary. Next, scoop the meat mixture and stuff each of the pepper halves. Top with cheddar cheese.

Place the stuffed pepper halves into the pot.

Close the crisping lid and press BAKE/ROAST. Set the temperature to 360°F and the time to 15 minutes. Press START/STOP to begin.

When cooking is finished, remove the pepper halves and serve immediately.

TURKEY CHILI

SERVES 6

2 TABLESPOONS GRAPESEED OIL

1 WHITE ONION, PEELED AND
  DICED

1 POUND LEAN GROUND TURKEY
  (OR ½ POUND LEAN GROUND
  TURKEY AND ½ POUND LEAN
  TURKEY SAUSAGE)

15 OUNCES RED KIDNEY BEANS,
  DRAINED

15 OUNCES San Marzano
  DICED TOMATOES

8 OUNCES San Marzano
  PUREED TOMATOES

1 TABLESPOON GARLIC, PEELED
  AND MINCED

1 TEASPOON CUMIN

¼ TEASPOON SALT

¼ TEASPOON GARLIC POWDER

¼ TEASPOON SMOKED PAPRIKA

¼ TEASPOON OREGANO

½ CUP LOW-SODIUM BEEF
  STOCK

Add the oil, onion, and ground turkey to the cooking pot. Stir well to combine.

Secure the pressure lid and turn the pressure-release valve to the SEAL position. Select SEAR/SAUTÉ and set to HIGH. Press START/STOP to begin. Cook until the ground turkey is no longer pink. Press START/STOP to turn off appliance.

Open the pressure lid and add the kidney beans, diced tomatoes, pureed tomatoes, garlic, cumin, salt, garlic powder, paprika, oregano, and beef stock. Secure the pressure lid and turn the pressure-release valve to the SEAL position. Select SEAR/SAUTÉ and set to HIGH for 10 minutes. Press START/STOP to begin.

When cooking is complete, turn the pressure-release valve to the VENT position. Wait until the pressure has been released, then remove the pressure lid.

Serve immediately with your desired chili toppings, such as shredded cheese, sour cream, and sliced scallions or chives.

Holiday Parties and Weekend Gatherings

ASIAN CHICKEN WINGS

SERVES 4 TO 6

2 CUPS WATER

1 POUND CHICKEN WINGS

1 TEASPOON SALT, DIVIDED

¼ CUP HONEY

½ CUP RICE WINE VINEGAR

2 TEASPOONS RED CHILI PEPPER
   PASTE

1 TEASPOON FRESH GINGER,
   GRATED

1 ORANGE, JUICED AND ZESTED

GREEN ONIONS, AS NEEDED,
   SLICED FOR GARNISH

Add the water to the cooking pot. Add the reversible rack in the pot, in the lower position. Arrange the wings on top of the rack.

Secure the pressure lid and turn the pressure-release valve to the SEAL position. Select PRESSURE and set to HIGH. Set the time to 2 minutes. Press START/STOP to begin.

After 2 minutes, turn the pressure-release valve to the VENT position. Wait until the pressure has been released, then remove the pressure lid.

Dry the wings with paper towels and season with ½ teaspoon salt.

In a mixing bowl, add the remaining salt, honey, rice wine vinegar, red chili pepper paste, ginger, and orange juice and zest. Whisk well to combine. Add the sauce to the cooking pot.

Return the reversible rack in the pot, in the lower position. Arrange the wings back on top of the rack.

Close the crisping lid and press AIR CRISP. Set the temperature to 390°F and the time to 30 minutes. Press START/STOP to begin. Turn the wings every 10 minutes until golden brown.

When cooking is finished, remove the wings and add to the pot. Toss well in the sauce until the wings are well coated. Remove and let cool slightly before serving. Garnish with sliced green onion.

ASIAN PORK SLIDERS
WITH PICKLED VEGETABLES

SERVES 8 TO 12

3 CUPS WATER

1 CUP RICE WINE VINEGAR

¼ CUP SUGAR

1½ TEASPOONS RED PEPPER
FLAKES

½ TABLESPOON SALT

2½ POUNDS BONELESS PORK
SHOULDER

1 TEASPOON FRESH GINGER,
GRATED

1 TEASPOON GARLIC, PEELED
AND MINCED

1½ TABLESPOONS AGAVE
NECTAR

1 TABLESPOON RED CHILI
PEPPER PASTE

¼ CUP ORANGE JUICE

STEAMED BUNS, AS NEEDED

PICKLED VEGETABLES, AS
NEEDED (SEE FOLLOWING
PAGE)

Add the water, vinegar, sugar, red pepper flakes, and salt to the cooking pot. Stir well and add the pork shoulder.

Secure the pressure lid and turn the pressure-release valve to the SEAL position.

Select PRESSURE and set to HIGH. Set the time to 90 minutes. Press START/STOP to begin.

After 90 minutes, turn the pressure-release valve to the VENT position. Wait until the pressure has been released, then remove the pressure lid.

Strain the liquid from the pot, reserving ½ cup of the liquid. Shred the pork and place back in the pot. Add the reserved liquid along with the ginger, garlic, agave nectar, red chili pepper paste, and orange juice.

Select SEAR/SAUTÉ and set to MEDIUM-HIGH. Allow the pork to simmer, uncovered, for 10 minutes or until the liquid is reduced, stirring occasionally.

Remove the shredded pork from the pot and serve on steamed buns with pickled vegetables

PICKLED VEGETABLES

½ CUP WARM WATER

1 TEASPOON SUGAR

½ CUP RICE WINE VINEGAR

1 TEASPOON FRESH GINGER, GRATED

½ RED ONION, THINLY SLICED

1 CARROT, PEELED AND THINLY SLICED ON THE BIAS

1 RED BELL PEPPER, SEEDED AND THINLY SLICED

In a mixing bowl, add the water, sugar, and vinegar. Stir until the sugar is dissolved.

Fill a suitable sealable glass container with the ginger, onion, carrot, and bell pepper. Pour the warm liquid over the top so all the vegetables are covered. Seal tightly and store in the refrigerator at least one hour, or overnight.

BARBECUE BAKED BEANS

SERVES 4 TO 6

8 OUNCES SMOKED BACON,
DICED

2 CUPS WHITE ONION, PEELED
AND DICED

3⅓ CUPS RED BEANS, RINSED

2 TEASPOONS SALT

2 TEASPOONS GARLIC SALT

3 TEASPOONS ONION POWDER

3½ CUPS WATER

1¾ CUPS BROWN SUGAR

15 OUNCES SAN MARZANO
PUREED TOMATOES

½ CUP APPLE CIDER VINEGAR

Add the diced bacon and onion to the cooking pot.

Select SEAR/SAUTÉ and set to HIGH for 10 minutes. Press START/STOP to begin. Note: You will not be using a lid until instructed.

When cooking is complete, add the beans, salt, garlic salt, onion powder, and water. Note: The beans should be covered with water.

Secure the pressure lid and turn the pressure-release valve to the SEAL position. Select PRESSURE and set to HIGH. Set the time to 60 minutes. Press START/STOP to begin.

When cooking is complete, allow the pressure to naturally release for 33 minutes. After 33 minutes, switch the valve to the VENT position. Wait until the pressure has been released, then remove the pressure lid.

Add the brown sugar, tomatoes, and apple cider vinegar. Stir well until incorporated into the beans.

Secure the crisping lid. Select BAKE/ROAST and set the temperature to 325°F for 45 minutes. Press START/STOP to begin. Stir about every 15 minutes.

When cooking is complete, remove the beans and serve immediately.

BARBECUE RIBS

SERVES 2 TO 4

1 FULL RACK PORK RIBS
(SILVERSKIN REMOVED)

¼ CUP SPICE RUB (YOUR
FAVORITE OR McCORMICK'S
BARBECUE SPICE)

2 TABLESPOONS SALT

2 TABLESPOONS BROWN SUGAR

½ CUP APPLE JUICE

1 CUP BARBECUE SAUCE (SEE
PAGE 100)

Place the rack on a large cutting board and cut the ribs into thirds.

In a small bowl, add the spice rub, salt, and brown sugar. Mix well, then season the racks liberally with the spice mixture.

Pour the apple juice into the cooking pot.

Place the racks into the cook and crisp basket, and place in the pot.

Secure the pressure lid and turn the pressure-release valve to the SEAL position. Select PRESSURE and set to HIGH. Set the time to 20 minutes. Press START/STOP to begin.

After 20 minutes, turn the pressure-release valve to the VENT position. Wait until the pressure has been released, then remove the pressure lid.

Close the crisping lid and press AIR CRISP. Set the temperature to 400°F and the time to 15 minutes. Press START/STOP to begin.

After 10 minutes, open the lid and brush the racks liberally with the barbecue sauce. Close the lid and continue to crisp for the remaining five minutes.

Cooking is finished when the internal temperature of the racks reaches 185°F. Use a kitchen thermometer to check.

Remove the ribs from the cook and crisp basket and let rest for 5 minutes before serving.

BARBECUE SAUCE

¾ CUP KETCHUP

1 TABLESPOON WHITE WINE
   VINEGAR

2 TEASPOONS SMOKED PAPRIKA

2 TABLESPOONS BROWN SUGAR

1 TABLESPOON
   WORCESTERSHIRE SAUCE

In a small bowl, add the ketchup, vinegar, smoked paprika, brown sugar, and Worcestershire sauce. Whisk until well combined. Refrigerate until ready to use.

BITE-SIZED CHICKEN CORN DOGS

SERVES 12 TO 14

1 ¼ CUPS ALL-PURPOSE FLOUR

¾ CUP CORN MEAL

¼ CUP SUGAR

2 TEASPOONS BAKING POWDER

½ TEASPOON SALT

1 CUP LOW-FAT MILK

1 EGG

4 CHICKEN (OR TURKEY) HOT
   DOGS, EACH CUT INTO 4
   EQUAL PIECES

1 ½ CUPS WATER

In a mixing bowl, add the flour, corn meal, sugar, baking powder, and salt. Mix well, then whisk in the milk and egg until a smooth batter is achieved.

Spray the inside of a Ninja accessory egg mold with nonstick spray. Pour the batter halfway into each mold. Push one hotdog piece into the center of each mold. Cover the mold with aluminum foil.

Pour the water into the cooking pot. Insert the reversible rack in the pot, in the lower position. Place the egg mold on top of the rack.

Secure the pressure lid and turn the pressure-release valve to the SEAL position. Select PRESSURE and set to HIGH. Set the time to 9 minutes. Press START/STOP to begin.

When cooking is complete, allow the pressure to naturally release for 5 minutes. Then, switch the valve to the VENT position. Wait until the pressure has been released, then remove the pressure lid.

Remove the foil and allow to cool for 3 to 4 minutes before gently flipping over the mold and gently pushing out the corn dog bites. Serve immediately with your favorite dipping sauces.

CHEESY DOUBLE-LAYER NACHOS

SERVES 6 TO 8

¼ BAG (4 OUNCES) TORTILLA
CHIPS, DIVIDED

12 OUNCES LOW-FAT MEXICAN
CHEESE BLEND, DIVIDED

8 OUNCES MEXICAN SALSA,
DIVIDED

GUACAMOLE, AS NEEDED, FOR
GARNISH

LOW-FAT SOUR CREAM, AS
NEEDED, FOR GARNISH

FRESH SCALLIONS, AS NEEDED,
FOR GARNISH

Arrange half of the tortilla chips in the cooking pot. Cover the chips with half of the cheese blend. Add half of the salsa evenly over the cheese and chips. Repeat with a second layer of the remaining tortilla chips topped with the remaining cheese and salsa.

Close the crisping lid and press AIR CRISP. Set the temperature to 360°F and the time to 5 minutes. Press START/STOP to begin.

When cooking is finished, remove the nachos and garnish with guacamole, sour cream, and fresh scallions, if desired. Serve immediately.

CHICKEN FRANKFURTER CHILI CHEESE DOGS

SERVES 4

4 CHICKEN FRANKFURTERS

4 HOT DOG BUNS, TOASTED IF
   DESIRED

8 OUNCES TURKEY CHILI
   (SEE PAGE 87)

¼ CUP FINELY SHREDDED LOW-
   FAT CHEDDAR OR MONTEREY
   JACK CHEESE

Place the frankfurters in the cook and crisp basket and place in the cooking pot. Close the crisping lid and press AIR CRISP. Set the temperature to 375°F and the time to 6 to 8 minutes, depending on the desired crispness of the hotdogs. Press START/STOP to begin.

After cooking, remove the frankfurters and place them in the buns. Top with warmed chili and shredded cheese.

Return the dressed hot dogs to the crisping basket. Close the crisping lid and press AIR CRISP. Set the temperature to 375°F and the time to 4 minutes, or until the cheese is melted.

Remove the hot dogs and serve.

CHICKEN FRITTERS

SERVES 4

1 POUND BONELESS, SKINLESS
   CHICKEN BREASTS, DICED

¼ CUP SHREDDED PARMESAN
   CHEESE

¼ CUP SHREDDED LOW-FAT
   PROVOLONE CHEESE

1 TEASPOON GARLIC SALT

1 TEASPOON ONION POWDER

1 TEASPOON SALT

1 TEASPOON FRESH CRACKED
   BLACK PEPPER

3 SCALLIONS, DICED

½ CUP PANKO BREAD CRUMBS

1 TABLESPOON DILL

1 EGG

In a mixing bowl, add the chicken, Parmesan cheese, provolone cheese, garlic salt, onion powder, salt, pepper, scallions, bread crumbs, dill, and the egg. Mix well to combine. Then shape into fritter shapes (or small patties) and refrigerate for at least 30 minutes to set.

Place the fritters into the cook and crisp basket, and place in the cooking pot, in the higher position.

Close the crisping lid and press AIR CRISP. Set the temperature to 350°F and the time to 10 minutes. Press START/STOP to begin.

After 10 minutes, open the lid and remove the fritters. Serve with your favorite dipping sauce.

CHICKEN SANDWICHES

SERVES 4

1 CUP ALL-PURPOSE FLOUR

1 TEASPOON GARLIC SALT

1 TEASPOON SMOKED PAPRIKA

1 TEASPOON DRIED BASIL

1 TEASPOON SALT

1 TEASPOON FRESH CRACKED
   BLACK PEPPER

½ CUP LOW-FAT MILK

1 EGG

4 BONELESS, SKINLESS CHICKEN
   BREASTS

1 TABLESPOON GRAPESEED OIL

In a mixing bowl, add the flour, garlic salt, paprika, basil, salt, and pepper. Mix well to combine.

In a separate bowl, add the milk and egg. Whisk until well combined.

Dredge the chicken breasts in the seasoned flour, coating all sides. Shake off the excess. Then dredge the breasts in the egg wash. Return the breasts to the seasoned flour mixture and coat well, shaking off the excess.

Grease the cook and crisp basket with the grapeseed oil and arrange the breasts into the basket.

Close the crisping lid and press AIR CRISP. Set the temperature to 390°F and the time to 5 minutes to preheat the appliance. Press START/STOP to begin.

After 5 minutes, open the crisping lid and place the basket into the cooking pot, in the higher position. Close the crisping lid and press AIR CRISP. Set the temperature to 390°F and the time to 20 minutes. Press START/STOP to begin.

After 20 minutes, check the chicken to make sure it's cooked through (or has an internal temperature of 160°F).

Remove the breasts from the basket and serve on toasted buns with your favorite fixings and toppings.

HOT BUFFALO WINGS

SERVES 4 TO 6

1 CUP WATER

2½ POUNDS FROZEN CHICKEN
   WINGS

1 STICK UNSALTED BUTTER,
   MELTED

1 CUP FRANK'S REDHOT® SAUCE

Pour the water into the cooking pot.

Place the chicken wings into the cook and crisp basket, and place in the pot.

Secure the pressure lid and turn the pressure-release valve to the SEAL position. Select PRESSURE and set to HIGH. Set the time to 10 minutes. Press START/STOP to begin.

After 10 minutes, turn the pressure-release valve to the VENT position. Wait until the pressure has been released, then remove the pressure lid.

Close the crisping lid and press AIR CRISP. Set the temperature to 400°F and the time to 20 minutes. Press START/STOP to begin. Open every 5 minutes to check for doneness.

In a large bowl, add the melted butter and hot sauce. Mix well to combine.

When cooking is finished, remove the wings and transfer them to the bowl. Toss well with the melted butter and hot sauce to coat and serve immediately.

SOUTH-OF-THE-BORDER STREET TACOS

SERVES 6 TO 8

½ CUP ORANGE JUICE

¼ CUP LIME JUICE

4 GARLIC CLOVES, PEELED AND
   DICED

1 CUP FRESH CILANTRO LEAVES

1 DRIED ANCHO CHILI, CHOPPED

1½ POUNDS SKIRT STEAK

1 CUP LOW-SODIUM BEEF STOCK

16 CORN TORTILLAS

4 OUNCES COTIJA CHEESE

FRESH CILANTRO, AS NEEDED,
   FOR GARNISH

1 CUP WHITE ONION, PEELED
   AND DICED, FOR GARNISH

½ CUP THINLY SLICED
   RADISHES, FOR GARNISH

½ CUP SLICED PICKLED
   JALAPEÑOS, FOR GARNISH

In a mixing bowl, add the orange juice, lime juice, garlic, cilantro, and ancho chili. Mix well, then pour into a large sealable plastic bag or suitable container. Add the skirt steak and allow to marinate for at least 4 hours, or overnight.

Add the marinade and steak to the cooking pot. Add the beef stock.

Secure the pressure lid and turn the pressure-release valve to the SEAL position. Select PRESSURE and set to HIGH. Set the time to 10 minutes. Press START/STOP to begin.

When cooking is complete, allow the pressure to naturally release for 10 minutes. Then, switch the valve to the VENT position. Wait until the pressure has been released, then remove the pressure lid.

Add the reversible rack to the pot, set in the higher position. Add the corn tortillas to the rack.

Close the crisping lid and press BROIL for 3 minutes. Press START/STOP to begin.

When finished, remove the corn tortillas and keep warm. Remove the steak and slice in strips against the grain (or simply chop the meat into small pieces).

Add the meat to the tortillas and top with the crumbled cheese. Garnish with the fresh cilantro and diced onions. Serve with sliced radishes and jalapeños on the side.

SOUTHERN FRIED PICKLES

SERVES 4

¼ CUP FLOUR (SEASONED WITH
SALT AND FRESH CRACKED
BLACK PEPPER)

⅛ TEASPOON BAKING POWDER

3 TABLESPOONS CARBONATED
WATER

⅛ TEASPOON SALT

2 TABLESPOONS WATER

2 TABLESPOONS CORNSTARCH

1½ CUPS PANKO BREAD CRUMBS

1 TEASPOON SMOKED PAPRIKA

1 TEASPOON GARLIC SALT

¼ TEASPOON CAYENNE PEPPER

25–30 DILL PICKLE SLICES,
SLICED ON THE BIAS, ABOUT
¼ INCH THICK, PATTED DRY

VEGETABLE OIL, AS NEEDED

RANCH DRESSING, FOR SERVING

DILL SAUCE, FOR SERVING

In a mixing bowl, add the flour, baking powder, carbonated water, salt, and water. Whisk well until a batter is achieved.

In a separate bowl, add the cornstarch. In another bowl, combine the bread crumbs, smoked paprika, garlic salt, and cayenne pepper.

Add the pickle slices to the cornstarch bowl. Toss well until the slices are well coated. Shake off any excess. Add the pickle slices to the bowl with the batter. Mix until slices are well coated. Remove the slices and add to the bowl with the seasoned bread crumbs. Toss well and shake off the excess bread crumb mixture.

Grease the cook and crisp basket with the oil and place the basket into the appliance. Close the crisping lid. Preheat by pressing AIR CRISP. Set temperature to 360°F for 3 minutes. Press START/STOP to begin.

After 3 minutes, open the crisping lid. Arrange the breaded pickle slices in the crisper basket. Close the crisping lid and select AIR CRISP. Set the temperature to 360°F for 10 minutes. Press START/STOP to begin.

After 5 minutes, open the crisping lid and press START/PAUSE to pause cooking. Remove the basket and turn the pickles over. Return the basket and press START/PAUSE to continue cooking.

When cooking is finished, remove the basket and pickles and serve immediately with ranch dressing or a dill sauce.

SWEET AND ZESTY CHICKEN WINGS

SERVES 4 TO 6

½ CUP WATER

3 POUNDS FROZEN CHICKEN
   WINGS

2 TABLESPOONS BROWN SUGAR

2 TEASPOONS GARLIC POWDER

2 TEASPOONS ONION POWDER

2 TEASPOONS SMOKED PAPRIKA

2 TEASPOONS CUMIN

1 TABLESPOON FRESH
   CILANTRO, MINCED

1 TEASPOON LIME ZEST

2 TABLESPOONS VEGETABLE OIL

Pour the water into the cooking pot.

Place the chicken wings into the cook and crisp basket and place the basket in the pot.

Secure the pressure lid and turn the pressure-release valve to the SEAL position. Select PRESSURE and set to HIGH. Set the time to 5 minutes. Press START/STOP to begin.

After 5 minutes, turn the pressure-release valve to the VENT position. Wait until the pressure has been released, then remove the pressure lid.

Remove the wings and pat dry with paper towels.

In a mixing bowl, add the brown sugar, garlic powder, onion powder, smoked paprika, cumin, cilantro, and lime zest. Mix well to combine.

Toss the wings with the vegetable oil, and then coat them in the sweet and zesty spice mixture. Return the wings to the basket.

Close the crisping lid and press AIR CRISP. Set the temperature to 390°F and the time to 15 minutes. Press START/STOP to begin.

After 8 minutes, open the lid and toss the wings with a pair of kitchen tongs to move them around. Close the lid and continue to crisp for the remaining 7 minutes.

When cooking is finished, remove the wings and transfer them to a platter. Serve immediately.

Breads, Sweets, and Treats

BAKED APPLES

SERVES 4

2 OR 3 CRISP APPLES

GROUND CINNAMON, TO TASTE

BROWN SUGAR, TO TASTE

3 CUPS WATER

VANILLA ICE CREAM, FOR
    SERVING

Slice the apples in wedges, removing the core. Sprinkle each slice with cinnamon and arrange the slices in a multipurpose baking pan. Sprinkle the brown sugar over the apples in the pan.

Pour the water into the bottom of the cooking pot. Place the pan of apples on the reversible rack, making sure the rack is in the lowest position in the pot.

Close the crisping lid, press BAKE/ROAST, and set the temperature to 375°F and the time to 10 to 12 minutes. Press START/STOP to begin.

When cooking is complete, check the apples for doneness. They may require an additional 5 minutes cooking time. Remove the apples and let cool slightly. Serve with vanilla ice cream, if desired.

BANANAS FOSTER

SERVES 2

1 TABLESPOON SALTED BUTTER, MELTED

1 TABLESPOON BROWN SUGAR

1 TABLESPOON CRÈME DE BANANA

½ TEASPOON LEMON ZEST

1 TEASPOON ORANGE ZEST

1 TABLESPOON ORANGE JUICE

1 LARGE RIPE BANANA, PEELED AND CUT INTO ½-INCH SLICES

1 TABLESPOON RUM

1 CUP VANILLA ICE CREAM

Close the crisping lid. Preheat the appliance for 5 minutes by pressing SEAR/SAUTÉ and set to MEDIUM-HIGH. Press START/STOP to begin.

After 5 minutes, add the butter, brown sugar, crème de banana, lemon zest, orange zest, and orange juice to the cooking pot. Stir until the butter and sugar has dissolved. Add the banana to the pot and cover with the mixture. Cook until the banana begins to soften and the mixture begins to bubble. Stir in the rum and cook for an additional 2 minutes.

After 2 minutes, press START/STOP to turn off the appliance. Immediately serve the bananas and mixture over ice cream.

BLUEBERRY AND NECTARINE COBBLER

SERVES 6

2 CUPS BLUEBERRIES

4 CUPS NECTARINES, SLICED

⅓ CUP LEMON JUICE

1 LEMON, ZESTED

⅔ CUP SUGAR

5 TABLESPOONS CORNSTARCH

1 TEASPOON CINNAMON

2 CUPS WATER

CRUMBLE

1½ CUPS ALL-PURPOSE FLOUR

1 CUP BROWN SUGAR

1 TABLESPOON CINNAMON

¼ TEASPOON SALT

⅔ CUP UNSALTED BUTTER,
   MELTED

1½ TEASPOONS VANILLA
   EXTRACT

Arrange the blueberries and nectarines in an 8-inch baking pan.

In a bowl, add the lemon juice, lemon zest, sugar, cornstarch, and cinnamon. Mix well to combine, then pour over the fruit in the pan.

Pour the water into the cooking pot, and place the reversible rack in the pot, in the lower position. Place the pan on top of the rack.

Secure the pressure lid and turn the pressure-release valve to the SEAL position. Select PRESSURE and set to HIGH. Set the time to 7 minutes. Press START/STOP to begin.

To make the crumble, combine the flour, brown sugar, cinnamon, and salt in a bowl. Add the melted butter and vanilla and continue to stir to combine.

When cooking is complete, allow the pressure to naturally release for 10 minutes. Then, switch the valve to the VENT position. Wait until the pressure has been released, then remove the pressure lid.

Stir the fruit mixture and let rest in the pot for 10 to 15 minutes, or until thick. Add the crumble evenly to the top of the mixture.

Close the crisping lid. Press AIR CRISP and set the temperature to 350°F and the time to 10 minutes. Press START/STOP to begin. Cook until top is brown and fruit is bubbling.

After 10 minutes, remove the pan and let cool before serving.

CHERRIES JUBILEE

SERVES 2

1 TABLESPOON SALTED BUTTER, MELTED

1 TABLESPOON SUGAR

1 TABLESPOON CHERRY LIQUEUR (*KIRSHWASSER*)

½ TEASPOON LEMON ZEST

¾ TABLESPOON LEMON JUICE

1 TEASPOON ORANGE ZEST

½ TABLESPOON ORANGE JUICE

12 FRESH WHOLE PITTED BLACK CHERRIES

1 TABLESPOON RUM

1 CUP VANILLA ICE CREAM

Close the crisping lid. Preheat the appliance for 5 minutes by pressing SEAR/SAUTÉ and set to MEDIUM-HIGH. Press START/STOP to begin.

After 5 minutes, add the butter, sugar, cherry liqueur, lemon zest, lemon juice, orange zest, and orange juice to the cooking pot. Stir until the butter and sugar have dissolved. Add the cherries to the pot and cover with the mixture. Cook until the cherries begin to soften and the mixture begins to bubble. Stir in the rum and cook for an additional 2 minutes.

After 2 minutes, press START/STOP to turn off the appliance. Immediately serve the cherries and mixture over ice cream.

CHERRY AND NECTARINE COBBLER

SERVES 6

1 CUP WHOLE PITTED BLACK

    CHERRIES

4 CUPS NECTARINES, SLICED

1 TEASPOON LEMON JUICE

3 TABLESPOONS SUGAR

2 TABLESPOONS CORNSTARCH

1 CUP WATER, DIVIDED

CRUMBLE

½ CUP ALL-PURPOSE FLOUR

½ CUP ROLLED OATS

⅔ CUP BROWN SUGAR

2 TABLESPOONS SUGAR

⅓ CUP UNSALTED BUTTER

1 TEASPOON CINNAMON

Arrange the cherries and nectarines in an 8-inch baking pan.

In a bowl, add the lemon juice, sugar, cornstarch, and ½ cup water. Mix well to combine, then pour over the fruit in the pan.

Pour the water into the cooking pot, and place the reversible rack in the pot, in the lower position. Place the pan on top of the rack and cover with aluminum foil.

Secure the pressure lid and turn the pressure-release valve to the SEAL position. Select PRESSURE and set to HIGH. Set the time to 10 minutes. Press START/STOP to begin.

To make the crumble, combine the flour, oats, brown sugar, sugar, butter, and cinnamon in a bowl.

After 10 minutes, turn the pressure-release valve to the VENT position. Wait until the pressure has been released, then remove the pressure lid.

Remove the foil and add the crumble evenly to the top of the fruit mixture.

Close the crisping lid. Preheat the appliance by pressing AIR CRISP and set the temperature to 400°F and the time for 12 minutes. Press START/STOP to begin. Cook until the top is brown and fruit is bubbling.

After 12 minutes, remove the pan and let cool before serving.

CHOCOLATE CHIP COOKIE SQUARES

SERVES 4 TO 6

1 CUP + 2 TABLESPOONS ALL-
PURPOSE FLOUR

½ TEASPOON BAKING SODA

½ TEASPOON SALT

½ CUP UNSALTED BUTTER

6 TABLESPOONS SUGAR

6 TABLESPOONS BROWN SUGAR

½ TEASPOON VANILLA EXTRACT

1 EGG

1 CUP SEMISWEET CHOCOLATE
CHIPS

Close the crisping lid. Preheat the appliance by pressing BAKE/
ROAST and set the temperature to 325°F and the time to 5 minutes.
Press START/STOP to begin.

In a mixing bowl, sift together the flour, baking soda, and salt.

In a separate bowl, add the butter, sugar, brown sugar, and vanilla.
Mix until well combined. Add the egg and continue to mix until
incorporated.

Add the "wet" ingredients to the "dry" ingredients, about ⅓ at a time.
Mix well, being careful not to overmix. Lastly, fold in the chocolate
chips.

Grease an 8-inch baking pan and add the cookie dough. Place the
reversible rack in the cooking pot, in the lower position. Place the pan
on top of the rack.

Close the crisping lid. Press BAKE/ROAST and set the temperature to
325°F and the time to 23 minutes. Press START/STOP to begin.

After 23 minutes, remove the pan and allow the cookies to cool for
5 minutes. Then remove the cookie from the pan and cut into
squares. Serve warm.

CLASSIC CARROT CAKE

SERVES 6

1 BOX CARROT CAKE MIX
  (DUNCAN HINES® DECADENT
  CLASSIC CARROT)
1¼ CUPS HOT WATER
¼ CUP VEGETABLE OIL
3 EGGS
1½ CUPS WATER
DUNCAN HINES® CREAM
  CHEESE CREAMY HOME-
  STYLE FROSTING

In a small bowl, add the carrots and raisins from the cake mix. Add the hot water and set aside for 5 minutes.

Using a stand mixer, combine in the bowl the cake mix, oil, eggs, and the carrot and raisin mixture (including any unabsorbed water). Beat by hand until well blended.

Pour the 1½ cups of water in the bottom of the cooking pot. Place the reversible rack into the pot, in the lower position.

Pour the cake batter into a greased 8-inch baking pan. Do not fill more than ¾ with batter. Cover the pan with aluminum foil and place on top of the rack.

Secure the pressure lid and turn the pressure-release valve to the SEAL position. Select PRESSURE and set to HIGH. Set the time to 27 minutes. Press START/STOP to begin.

After 27 minutes, turn the pressure-release valve to the VENT position. Wait until the pressure has been released, then remove the pressure lid.

Carefully remove the cake by removing the foil and flipping over the pan. Allow to cool completely before frosting. Slice and serve.

COCONUT SUPREME CAKE

SERVES 6

1 BOX COCONUT CAKE MIX
(DUNCAN HINES® COCONUT
SUPREME)

2 CUPS WATER, DIVIDED

⅓ CUP UNSWEETENED
APPLESAUCE

3 EGG WHITES

DUNCAN HINES® WHIPPED
FLUFFY WHITE FROSTING
(OPTIONAL)

Using a stand mixer, combine in the bowl the cake mix, ¾ cup water, applesauce, and the egg whites. Mix on low speed until moistened, then beat for 2 minutes.

Pour the remaining 1½ cups of water in the bottom of the cooking pot. Place the reversible rack into the pot, in the lower position.

Pour the cake batter into a greased 8-inch baking pan. Do not fill more than ¾ with batter. Cover the pan with aluminum foil and place on the top of the rack.

Secure the pressure lid and turn the pressure-release valve to the SEAL position. Select PRESSURE and set to HIGH. Set the time to 27 minutes. Press START/STOP to begin.

After 27 minutes, turn the pressure-release valve to the VENT position. Wait until the pressure has been released, then remove the pressure lid.

Carefully remove the cake by removing the foil and flipping over the pan. Allow to cool completely before frosting, if desired. Slice and serve.

HEARTY LOW-CARB CHEDDAR BISCUITS

SERVES 8 TO 10

2 CUPS CARBQUIK™ COMPLETE
   BISCUIT AND BAKING MIX)
2 OUNCES COLD, UNSALTED
   BUTTER
½ TEASPOON SEA SALT
½ TEASPOON GARLIC SALT
½ TEASPOON ONION POWDER
¼ CUP WATER
¼ CUP HEAVY CREAM
½ CUP LOW-FAT SHREDDED
   CHEDDAR CHEESE

In a bowl of a stand mixer, add the Carbquik and butter, and pulse until combined. Add the salt, garlic salt, and onion powder and continue to pulse to mix. Add the dough attachment along with the water and cream. Continue to mix until a dough forms. Note: Add more water if dough batter is dry. Add the cheese.

Remove the dough and shape into 8 to 10 biscuits.

Place the cook and crisp basket in the cooking pot and add the biscuits.

Close the crisping lid. Press AIR CRISP and set the temperature to 400°F and the time for 8 minutes. Press START/STOP to begin.

After 8 minutes, check the biscuits for doneness. Turn the biscuits over and continue to cook for another 1 or 2 minutes, or until golden brown and flaky.

When cooking is complete, remove the biscuits from the basket and serve warm.

JALAPEÑO CHEDDAR CORN BREAD

SERVES 8

1¼ CUPS ALL-PURPOSE FLOUR

¾ CUP CORNMEAL

¼ CUP SUGAR

2 TEASPOONS BAKING POWDER

2 TEASPOONS SALT

1 EGG

1 CUP LOW-FAT MILK

¼ CUP VEGETABLE OIL

1 LARGE JALAPEÑO, SEEDED AND
  DICED

1 CUP SHREDDED LOW-FAT
  CHEDDAR CHEESE

Place an 8-inch multipurpose baking pan on the reversible rack, making sure the rack is in the lower position in the cooking pot. Close the crisping lid. Preheat the appliance by pressing BROIL and set the time for 10 minutes. Press START/STOP to begin.

In a mixing bowl, sift the flour, cornmeal, sugar, baking powder, and salt together.

In another bowl, beat the egg with the milk, and vegetable oil. Add the sifted ingredients to the creamed mixture and beat well. Stir in the diced jalapeño and cheese until well combined.

Once preheated, grease the pan on the reversible rack, and pour in the batter. Close the crisping lid, press BAKE/ROAST, and set the temperature to 350°F and the time to 20 minutes. Press START/STOP to begin.

Cooking is complete when a toothpick inserted in the center of the corn bread comes out clean. Remove the pan from the pot and place on a cooling rack. Let cool for about 5 minutes before serving.

OLD-FASHIONED APPLE FRUIT PIES

SERVES 8

DOUGH:

1¼ CUPS ALL-
PURPOSE FLOUR

½ TEASPOON SALT

½ TEASPOON SUGAR

½ CUP UNSALTED
BUTTER, CUT IN
CUBES

2–3 TABLESPOONS ICE
WATER

FILLING:

1–2 FRESH GREEN
APPLES (GRANNY
SMITH), PEELED,
CORED, AND DICED

1 TEASPOON LEMON
JUICE

1 TABLESPOON SUGAR

½ TABLESPOON
CINNAMON

2 TABLESPOONS
TOFFEE

1 EGG

1 TABLESPOON WATER

In a food processor, add the flour, salt, and sugar and pulse to combine. Then add the butter and pulse until the mixture is coarse. Add the water and pulse until a dough-like mixture is achieved. Note: You may need to add additional water.

Place the dough on a floured surface and roll into a large disk. Wrap in plastic wrap and refrigerate for at least 30 minutes.

Make the filling by combining the apples, lemon juice, sugar, cinnamon, and toffee in a mixing bowl. Mix well to combine.

In a separate bowl, combine the egg and water. Whisk well to make the egg wash.

Place the cook and crisp basket in the cooking pot.

Close the crisping lid. Preheat the appliance by pressing AIR CRISP and set the temperature to 325°F and the time to 5 minutes. Press START/STOP to begin.

Remove the dough from the refrigerator and roll out onto a floured surface. Using a 3-inch round biscuit cutter (you can also use the bottom of a large drinking glass), cut out 16 disks of dough. Note: For larger pies, cut large circles of 8 disks of dough, which will be folded over to form each pie.

Place 1 or 2 teaspoons of fruit filling in the center of 8 dough circle (or on one side if making larger pies). Brush the edges of each dough circle with the egg wash. Top each circle with another dough circle (or fold over the dough if making larger pies) and seal the edges, using a fork as a crimp. Brush the tops of each pie with the egg wash.

Note: You can also make mini-pies (pictured) by creating small crusts that you can fill, followed by crimping a flat disk of dough to seal the top.

Open the crisping lid and, cooking in batches, add 4 pies to the basket in an even layer. Press AIR CRISP and set the temperature to 325°F and the time for 12 minutes. Press START/STOP to begin.

After 8 minutes, open the crisping lid and turn the pies over. Close the lid and continue to cook.

When cooking is complete, remove the pies and cook the remaining pies. Let cool before serving.

SAN FRANCISCO SOURDOUGH BREAD

MAKES 1 LOAF

1½ CUPS WARM WATER, DIVIDED

1½ TEASPOONS ACTIVE DRY YEAST

1 TEASPOON SUGAR

3 CUPS ALL-PURPOSE FLOUR

1 CUP PLAIN YOGURT

2 TEASPOONS SEA SALT

In the bowl of a stand mixer, add ½ cup of the warm water, and mix for about 5 minutes with the yeast and sugar. The mixture should be foamy. Next, add the dough attachment, and add the flour, yogurt, and salt. Mix on medium-low speed for about 2 minutes, or until the dough forms. Using a rubber spatula, scrape down the sides of the bowl, and then continue to mix on medium speed for about 5 more minutes.

Close the crisping lid. Preheat the appliance by pressing BAKE/ROAST and set the temperature to 250°F and the time to 1 minute. Press START/STOP to begin.

Shape the dough into a ball and place in the warm pot and cover with a small kitchen towel. Let the dough "rest" until it doubles in size, about 2 hours. Then remove and transfer to a floured surface. Reform into a ball. Grease the reversible rack and place the dough on top of the rack. Pour the remaining water in the pot. Then, place the rack in the pot, in the lower position. Cover again with the kitchen towel and let rest for 15 minutes. Using a sharp knife, make a "crisscross" mark on top of the dough, about ½-inch deep.

Close the crisping lid. Preheat the appliance by pressing BAKE/ROAST and set the temperature to 325°F and the time to 40 minutes. Press START/STOP to begin.

After 40 minutes, the loaf should be browned and the bottom fully baked. Remove from the rack and allow to cool before serving.

ZUCCHINI BREAD

MAKES 1 LOAF

3 CUPS ALL-PURPOSE FLOUR

1 TEASPOON SALT

1 TEASPOON BAKING SODA

1 TEASPOON BAKING POWDER

1 TABLESPOON GROUND
   CINNAMON

3 EGGS

1 CUP VEGETABLE OIL

2¼ CUPS SUGAR

3 TEASPOONS VANILLA EXTRACT

2 CUPS ZUCCHINI, GRATED

1 CUP CHOPPED WALNUTS

Close the crisping lid. Preheat the appliance by pressing BAKE/ROAST and set the temperature to 325°F and the time to 5 minutes. Press START/STOP to begin. In a mixing bowl, sift the flour, salt, baking soda, baking powder, and cinnamon together. In another bowl, beat the eggs with the vegetable oil, sugar, and vanilla. Add the sifted ingredients to the creamed mixture and beat well. Stir in the zucchini and nuts until well combined. Grease an 8-inch baking pan and add the batter to the pan.

Once preheated, place the pan on the reversible rack, making sure the rack is in the lower position in the cooking pot. Close the crisping lid, press BAKE/ROAST, and set the temperature to 325°F and the time to 40 minutes. Press START/STOP to begin. Cooking is complete when a toothpick inserted in the center of the bread comes out clean. Remove the pan from the pot and place on a cooling rack. Let cool for about 20 minutes before serving.

ABOUT THE AUTHORS

James O. Fraioli is an accomplished cookbook author with a James Beard Award to his credit. He's published more than thirty celebrated culinary books, which have been featured on Food Network, *The Ellen DeGeneres Show*, Martha Stewart Living Radio, in *O, The Oprah Magazine*, *Vogue*, *Forbes*, the *Wall Street Journal*, and *The New York Times*. He's best known for teaming up with chefs, restaurants, mixologists, and industry professionals to showcase the best the culinary world has to offer. Prior to his successful culinary book publishing career, James served as a contributing writer and editor for dozens of food and wine magazine publications. He resides just outside Seattle, Washington. Visit him online at culinarybookcreations.com.

Tiffany Fraioli has more than a decade of culinary and hospitality experience, hailing from the acclaimed Hawksworth Restaurant, located in the heart of downtown Vancouver inside the prestigious Rosewood Hotel Georgia.

Prior to Hawksworth, Tiffany was an integral part of the opening team of Chef Angus An's award-winning Maenam Restaurant in the heart of Kitsilano.

Tiffany's passion for the exciting culinary and hospitality industry started with an opportunity in 2008 when she was hired as part of the opening team to Chef Daniel Boulud's Lumiere and db Bistro Moderne.

Today, Tiffany works with husband James O. Fraioli and Culinary Book Creations, offering her assistance and skill in the areas of award-winning cookbooks, catering events, and much more.

INDEX

CONVERSION CHARTS

METRIC AND IMPERIAL CONVERSIONS

(These conversions are rounded for convenience)

Ingredient	Cups/Tablespoons/Teaspoons	Ounces	Grams/Milliliters
Butter	1 cup/16 tablespoons/ 2 sticks	8 ounces	230 grams
Cheese, shredded	1 cup	4 ounces	110 grams
Cream cheese	1 tablespoon	0.5 ounce	14.5 grams
Cornstarch	1 tablespoon	0.3 ounce	8 grams
Flour, all-purpose	1 cup/1 tablespoon	4.5 ounces/0.3 ounce	125 grams/8 grams
Flour, whole wheat	1 cup	4 ounces	120 grams
Fruit, dried	1 cup	4 ounces	120 grams
Fruits or veggies, chopped	1 cup	5 to 7 ounces	145 to 200 grams
Fruits or veggies, pureed	1 cup	8.5 ounces	245 grams
Honey, maple syrup, or corn syrup	1 tablespoon	0.75 ounce	20 grams
Liquids: cream, milk, water, or juice	1 cup	8 fluid ounces	240 milliliters
Oats	1 cup	5.5 ounces	150 grams
Salt	1 teaspoon	0.2 ounce	6 grams
Spices: cinnamon, cloves, ginger, or nutmeg (ground)	1 teaspoon	0.2 ounce	5 milliliters
Sugar, brown, firmly packed	1 cup	7 ounces	200 grams
Sugar, white	1 cup/1 tablespoon	7 ounces/0.5 ounce	200 grams/12.5 grams
Vanilla extract	1 teaspoon	0.2 ounce	4 grams